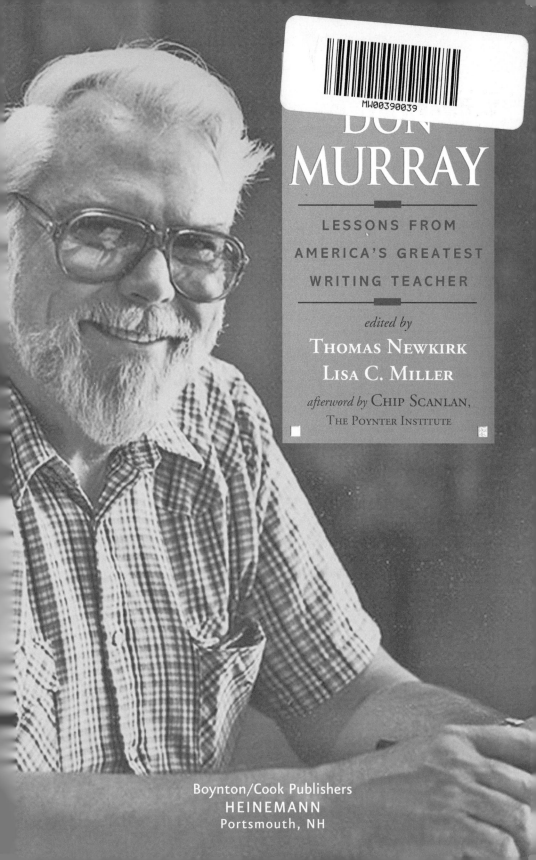

DON
MURRAY

LESSONS FROM
AMERICA'S GREATEST
WRITING TEACHER

edited by
THOMAS NEWKIRK
LISA C. MILLER

afterword by CHIP SCANLAN,
THE POYNTER INSTITUTE

Boynton/Cook Publishers
HEINEMANN
Portsmouth, NH

Boynton/Cook Publishers, Inc.
361 Hanover Street
Portsmouth, NH 03801–3912
www.boyntoncook.com

Offices and agents throughout the world

The editors and publisher wish to thank those who have generously given permission to reprint borrowed material:

Chapter 1: "Teach Writing as Process Not Product" by Donald Murray from *The Leaflet*, Fall 1972, pages 11–14. Published by the New England Association of Teachers of English. Reprinted by permission of the publisher.

Acknowledgments for borrowed material continue on p. viii.

Library of Congress Cataloging-in-Publication Data
The essential Don Murray : lessons from America's greatest writing teacher / Don Murray ; edited by Thomas Newkirk and Lisa C. Miller ; afterword by Chip Scanlan, Poynter Institute.
    p.   cm.
  Includes bibliographical references.
  ISBN-13: 978-0-86709-600-2
  ISBN-10: 0-86709-600-4
  1. English philology—Study and teaching. 2. English language—Rhetoric—Study and teaching. 3. Report writing—Study and teaching. 4. Journalism—Study and teaching. 5. Journalism—Authorship.   I. Newkirk, Thomas.
II. Miller, Lisa C.   III. Murray, Donald Morison, 1924–2006.

PE26.M87E88 2009
808'.04207—dc22   2009033950

Editor: Maura Sullivan
Production: Vicki Kasabian
Cover design: Lisa A. Fowler
Typesetter: Kim Arney
Manufacturing: Steve Bernier

Printed in the United States of America on acid-free paper
13 12   VP   2 3 4 5

To Donald Graves

*Dear friend of Don Murray and an inspiring educator
who changed the landscape of writing instruction—
and opened doors for us all*

Contents

Contents

Acknowledgments

WE WISH TO THANK CHIP SCANLAN, DON'S GOOD FRIEND AND WRITING colleague, who sponsored our visit to the Eugene Patterson Library at the Poynter Institute and also wrote the afterword for this book. We also thank Collection Development Librarian Jean Wood and Library Director David Shedden of Poynter, who helped us find what we needed from the more than 120 boxes that make up the Donald M. Murray Collection at the Institute. We owe special thanks to Jean, who pulled out columns, handouts, and more from the collection before we arrived, to make our job easier. Somehow, she managed to find exactly what we were looking for.

We deeply appreciate the way Heinemann has supported this project from the beginning. The original impetus came from Leigh Peake and her successor Maura Sullivan helped see the project through. Abby Heim and Vicki Kasabian did their usual masterful jobs of managing the production end, and we were fortunate for Lisa Fowler's artful work on the cover design. We also want to thank Sarah Gibbons and Sabina Foote for helping get the manuscript ready.

Introduction

You shall no longer take things at second or third hand, nor
look though the eyes of the dead, nor feed on the spectres
in books,

You shall not look through my eyes either, nor take things
from me,
You shall listen to all sides and filter them from yourself.
> —Walt Whitman, "Song of Myself"

IF DON MURRAY HAD BEEN ABLE TO HANG AROUND A COUPLE OF months after his death in December 2006, he would have been gratified by how much writing it called forth. There were the official obituaries, of course, but also hundreds of contributions to the websites of the University of New Hampshire journalism program and the Poynter Institute. He was a character, a giant, literally larger than life; for many of us he was the most public person we knew, an egotist to be sure, but one who made his life and writing processes so available to us. His stories called up our own. His obsession with writing stimulated us to put words on paper (or screen). And he offered these invitations to everyone, from writers on the *Boston Globe* to school lunch attendants who said they were interested in writing (he would invariably take their addresses and send them a packet of articles a couple days later). Grad students or sixth graders, it didn't matter. It was probably no exaggeration when Roy Peter Clark of the Poynter Institute called him "America's greatest writing teacher."

The title of this collection plays on the double meaning of *essential*. In one sense, we confidently make the claim that Donald Murray's writing is essential for all who are interested in the writing process. No one studied the writing process as obsessively as

Murray did, and no one wrote about it as eloquently and incisively. His very lucidity, we feel, may have caused some contemporary scholars to diminish the intellectual work that is represented in these essays. We hope that this collection will allow a new generation of writing teachers and aspiring writers to appreciate both the utility and depth of Don's work. We also believe that a healthy rereading of his work will establish his significance at a time when he has been marginalized by the field of composition that he helped create, an exclusion that he felt keenly in the last decade of his life. In one infamous rejection he was criticized for being too "Murrayesque."

In the late 1980s James Berlin put forward a taxonomy of composition rhetorics in which he claimed that each rhetoric has a tacit ideology—an often unspoken set of political orientations— that he was making explicit. Through a selective reading of Murray's work, he classified him as an Expressionist, with a focus on the inner reality of the writer, and a disregard for wider social realities. The intense individualism of expressionism, so the argument went, caused it to be politically ineffectual (an odd charge to make against someone who had won a Pulitzer Prize for editorial writing). In one version of this taxonomy, he claimed Murray was a Platonist because his belief in an inner reality the writer could somehow consult. Murray found this criticism so baffling, even incomprehensible, that he never really responded to it. Calling him a Platonist is a little like calling a garage door repairman an antinomian—probably untrue, but in any case not particularly relevant to the work he sets out to do.

When this taxonomy was first proposed, many of us felt confident that any fair reading of Murray (or the others in this category) would surely undermine the taxonomy. Unfortunately Berlin provided a convenient shorthand for conceptualizing the field, and the term stuck. It is beyond the scope of this introduction to make a full response here, but we believe that a reading of Don's work, which we hope we have represented fairly in this collection, will demonstrate the futility of such pigeonholing. Of course he is aware of a social dimension of composing. Of course he sees the writer operating in a system of genres that have their own histories and constraints. Of course the writer attends to an "other self" that reflects the voices and expectations of a wider public. No professional would claim the radical and irresponsible freedom to write according to some purely inner directive. And Don was, above all, a professional.

In fact, Don's mission, his calling, was to demystify writing by revealing as much as possible the communal habits, attitudes, and processes of practicing writers. In Frank Smith's phrase, he invited all who were interested to "join the club." There is an ancient saying that "the fox knows many things, but the hedgehog knows one big thing." In this sense, Murray was a hedgehog, obsessed with the knowable and the unknowable aspects of the composing process. All his life he collected the testimonies of writers, publishing a selection in *Shoptalk*. He was fascinated with the tools writers used—the right pen, the right-size notebook, and later, the right word processing program. (On a page of his daybook we have included a list of his favorite pens entitled, "Some pens I will follow.") He was notorious for adding program upon program to his software, crashing regularly. He was fascinated by writing schedules, writing productivity—for years he kept his own daily word counts which he shared with all of us. And practically everyone in Durham had a laminated strip with Pliny's maxim "Nulla Dies Sine Linea" that they received from Don.

Even more important were the generative accounts of the process itself. He began his work in composition at a time when outlines were king; when the thesis set rigid boundaries. The structure of a piece of writing resembled those elaborate hierarchical business structures at places like General Motors. The act of writing itself was depicted as little more than the implementation of a plan. The bestselling textbook from the 1950s, James McCrimmon's *Writing with a Purpose*, give this warning:

A student who clearly understands his purpose is not likely to be trapped by an accidental sequence of ideas, for he will recognize when he is going astray. A good deal of writing is censorship—keeping irrelevant thoughts out of the paper. Many of the ideas that arise in our minds have little relation to the purpose of our writing, and the habit of following impromptu ideas may result in a jumble of pointless remarks. (8)

For Murray, it was precisely this possibility of surprise that caused him to embrace these accidents. It was precisely this self-censorship that he encouraged his students to outrun.

His favorite piece of counsel was probably from William Stafford on the need to lower standards to allow writing to happen, which became almost a mantra to him. The job of the writer, Stafford argued, was to embrace a standard that allowed writing to happen; it required self-acceptance and a willingness to suspend judgment, to see where the process is leading. Murray had little (actually no) patience with those who claimed to be suffering writer's block—the writer was a workman like a plumber, or tree cutter, or roofer. Writer's block was as unprofessional as roofer's block or electrician's block. In one of his (many) versions of "A Writer's Canon" he advises, "Don't look back. Yes, the draft needs fixing. But first it needs writing."

Murray's own process was a complex mix of very orderly rituals and habits that allowed him to enter a state where he could be responsive to the suggestions of writing itself. As much as he worked to codify this advice, as much as he would define and redefine the elements of the writing process, it was the mystery of composing that ultimately attracted him. The evolving text was never, for Murray, purely a creation of the writer—it was an active participant in the process itself. He would speak of "listening to the text," or "the informing line"; he would describe the thrill of writing outrunning intention and entering new territory. This text itself was a player in the act of writing—*if* the writer was alert to cues and possibilities, and not tied to an outline or a plan. In his writing canon that we have included he assures us, "Be patient, listen quietly, the writing will come. The voice of the writing will tell you what to do." In the mysterious way that memory and association work, a single word could call up a whole new mental territory.

Proust writes about his famous madeleine and the entire world of Combray opens up to him.

Don's daybooks, bits of which we reproduce in this collection, were the starting point for almost all his sustained writing. During a workshop in the late 1980s he shared pages of them with a group of UNH teachers—we were each given a few pages and asked to respond in writing. Then someone else in the group would respond to the response. Tom was fortunate to be paired with Don himself, and even this short exchange between them suggests the complex generative view Don had of writing:

TN: A number of impressions come to mind. To write like this is to take your life seriously. To take memory seriously, to be obsessive, to take relationships seriously, to take impressions seriously. Many starts, minimal poems, many not fleshed out beyond that point. I like the mix of things in this—quotes clipped, poems pasted in, free drafts, papers delivered at conferences, and surrounding this work is his calculation and daily lists. Lists of all kinds. . . . Why lists? There is the freedom of order—there needs to be no structure. There is the generatively, one item leading to another. There is the illusion of control—things to do, crossed out as they are done.

There is in this work the paradox of control, a process of writing open to surprise, confined by, surrounded by, the forms that emphasize control. The poem next to the "to do" list. Maybe this, more than anything gets at the tension of the writer's life. Rigidity and openness, control and lack of control. . . .

DM: The idea that I take so many things seriously is insightful (interesting word for writing as visual—Art Book). It is obvious, as all truths—important truths—are but I never knew it before, not in that way.

And the tension between freedom and control—the necessity of control to achieve freedom, the way I take control seriously so I can escape it—burst through it. Again I never saw my need for control in that way—home, school, army, career—work against control—no freedom without control.

There was always something akin to the meditative practices of Eastern religions in the way Don approached writing; it was a mysterious opening up that could only occur amid a set of inflexible habits and procedures. There was something paradoxical and Taoist in his invitations to "know unknowing."

Another meaning of *essential* would imply that we, as editors, have been able to review all of his published and unpublished work and pull out the work that was truly enduring. We obviously have no such pretension, and could imagine one or more entirely different books that are just as essential (one hopes that his columns might be collected). In making our selection we created a few ground rules. The focus of the collection is on writing, which meant that we did not draw extensively from his columns (though we include one on Orwell) or the two memoirs he wrote. We also excluded sections of his textbooks, making only the exception of his exquisite essay, "I Still Wait for the Sheets to Move," which appeared in early versions of *Write to Learn*.

We begin with Don's groundbreaking essays "Teaching Writing as a Process Not Product" and "Writing as Process: How Writing Finds Its Own Meaning." Toward the end of "Writing as Process," he says:

> By the time this is published I will, I hope, have moved on. There are those who may be concerned by what they consider inconsistency or disloyalty to my own words. No matter, I have no choice. The pieces of writing I have not yet thought of writing will become different from what I expect them to be when I propose them to myself. My constant is change.

In a sense Don was both loyal and disloyal—loyal to his questions about the writing process, and disloyal to his provisional answers.

We found it impossible to split the book into sections, since there is so much overlap and connection between the parts. Change, surprise, and discovery are the threads that tie together all the work presented here. In the daybook pages he writes, "It must be fun to make this continual, daily book. Tonight I have rediscovered something of the wonder of writing—back to basics." Throughout the book he questions what he's known before and moves into new territory. He discusses delay and rehearsal, obstacles to getting writing done and ways to get past them, ways to listen to drafts, revision, and of course, ways to teach our students to do all of these. He takes us through his process, reseeing that process again and again—as does this book—from waiting and need to planning and drafting to the celebration he describes in "Where Was I Headed When I Left?" Always he comes back to what a writer is, what making writing is, as in "Getting Under the Lightning": "Writing is primarily not a matter of talent, of dedication, of vision, of vocabulary, of style, but simply a matter of sitting. The writer is a person who writes."

In the last essay in the book, "The Importance of Making Snow," he is back where he started, the magician who says, "There is always magic in this for me, and wonder because I do not know what I am going to say until it is said. The writer within is always a stranger, with a grin, a top hat and long, quick fingers which produce what was not there before. I shall never know this magic man well, although he has been within me for sixty years. He entices me with his capacity to surprise."

While our main focus was on his published essays, we did not want to be limited to that set of work—even though that would have made our job much easier. So much of his teaching was carried out in the form of handouts, one-pagers, excerpts from his daybooks, photocopies of the *New York Times* essays. In his last years he would host potluck dinners for grad students, and even those would come with handouts. We have collected some of these from former students and friends, and the Poynter Collection contained folder after folder of them. For a man in love with lists, the handout is a near-perfect genre. In assembling this book, we have interspersed these handouts, drawings, and daybook entries among the more recognizable published and anthologized essays. We found one of these handouts, given to Paul Matsuda's writing class, especially poignant. It sums up some of the enabling and disabling advice he has been given. In the latter category, labeled "The three stupidest things I've done as a writer," he mentions the belief that there is a hierarchy of genres:

> 1. [I] believed that there was an aesthetic genre hierarchy: 1. Poetry, 2. Literary fiction, 3. Essay of literary criticism, 4. Drama, 5. Popular fiction, 6. Screenwriting, 7. Essay of personal experience, 8. Journalism. At age 77 I realized that I am a storyteller who must tell the stories life has given me. The genre must come from the story to be told not from the literary ambition of the writer.

We suspect that even as he wrote this, late in his career, he had trouble believing it. For the last thirty years of his life he was working on a novel, which he never published, though he often wrote about it, and even gave readings from it. After all, he came of age as a writer when the true test of skill was the creation of an artful and successful novel. Many of us found it odd that someone so obsessed with deadlines and finishing would linger on a project so long. And we suspect that his failure to complete the book weighed on him.

But artfulness can take many forms, as he was trying to convince himself in this late handout. He virtually reinvented the academic essay, proving to all of us who followed him that one could be serious without being solemn. That academic writing could have voice and even humor. In the "The Listening Eye," for example, he imagines the shame of his colleagues discovering that he actually likes giving a writing conference where the student takes the lead:

> It doesn't seem possible to be an English teacher without the anxiety that I will be exposed by my colleagues. They will find out how little I do; my students will expose me to them; the English Department will line up in military formation in front of Hamilton Smith Hall and, after the buttons are cut off my Pendleton shirt, my university library card will be torn once across each way and let flutter to the ground.

No one before had written like this, in *College English*, no less.
He had made the choice to be an academic (attracted, he said, by
the health benefits), but he brought to his academic writing the
gifts of a skilled narrative writer, and his own irrepressible humor.
We would argue that the cumulative brilliance of these essays—
their artfulness, their humor, their deceptive complexity—may be
the best proof of Don's point about genre. In the lowly essay he
had found the place for exploring his great obsession—the writing
process.

nulla dies sine linea

Never a day without a line

– Horace 65-8 B.C.

one

Teach Writing as a
Process Not Product
(1972)

Most of us are trained as English teachers by studying a product: writing. Our critical skills are honed by examining literature, which is finished writing; language as it has been used by authors. And then, fully trained in the autopsy, we go out and are assigned to teach our students to write, to make language live.

Naturally we try to use our training. It's an investment and so we teach writing as a product, focusing our critical attentions on what our students have done, as if they had passed literature in to us. It isn't literature, of course, and we use our skills, with which we can dissect and sometimes almost destroy Shakespeare or Robert Lowell, to prove it.

Our students knew it wasn't literature when they passed it in, and our attack usually does little more than confirm their lack of self-respect for their work and for themselves; we are as frustrated as our students, for conscientious, doggedly responsible, repetitive autopsying doesn't give birth to live writing. The product doesn't improve, and so, blaming the student—who else?—we pass him along to the next teacher, who is trained, too often, the same way we were. Year after year the student shudders under a barrage of criticism, much of it brilliant, some of it stupid, and all of it irrelevant. No matter how careful our criticisms, they do not help the student since when we teach composition we are not teaching a product, we are teaching a process.

1

And once you can look at your composition program with the realization you are teaching a process, you may be able to design a curriculum which works. Not overnight, for writing is a demanding, intellectual process; but sooner than you think, for the process can be put to work to produce a product which may be worth your reading.

What is the process we should teach? It is the process of discovery through language. It is the process of exploration of what we should know and what we feel about what we know through language. It is the process of using language to learn about our world, to evaluate what we learn about our world, to communicate what we learn about our world.

Instead of teaching finished writing, we should teach unfinished writing, and glory in its unfinishedness. We work with language in action. We share with our students the continual excitement of choosing one word instead of another, of searching for the one true word.

This is not a question of correct or incorrect, of etiquette or custom. This is a matter of far higher importance. The writer, as he writes, is making ethical decisions. He doesn't test his words by a rule book, but by life. He uses language to reveal the truth to himself so that he can tell it to others. It is an exciting, eventful, evolving process.

This process of discovery through language we call writing can be introduced to your classroom as soon as you have a very simple understanding of that process, and as soon as you accept the full implications of teaching process, not product.

The writing process itself can be divided into three stages: *prewriting, writing,* and *rewriting.* The amount of time a writer spends in each stage depends on his personality, his work habits, his maturity as a craftsman, and the challenge of what he is trying to say. It is not a rigid lock-step process, but most writers most of the time pass through these three stages.

Prewriting is everything that takes place before the first draft. Prewriting usually takes about 85 percent of the writer's time. It includes the awareness of his world from which his subject is born. In prewriting, the writer focuses on that subject, spots an audience,

2

chooses a form which may carry his subject to his audience. Prewriting may include research and daydreaming, note-making and outlining, title-writing and lead-writing.

Writing is the act of producing a first draft. It is the fastest part of the process, and the most frightening, for it is a commitment. When you complete a draft you know how much, and how little, you know. And the writing of this first draft—rough, searching, unfinished—may take as little as one percent of the writer's time.

Rewriting is reconsideration of subject, form, and audience. It is researching, rethinking, redesigning, rewriting—and finally, line-by-line editing, the demanding, satisfying process of making each word right. It may take many times the hours required for a first draft, perhaps the remaining 14 percent of the time the writer spends on the project.

How do you motivate your student to pass through this process, perhaps even pass through it again and again on the same piece of writing?

First by shutting up. When you are talking he isn't writing. And you don't learn a process by talking about it, but by doing it. Next by placing the opportunity for discovery in your student's hands. When you give him an assignment you tell him what to say and how to say it, and thereby cheat your student of the opportunity to learn the process of discovery we call writing.

To be a teacher of a process such as this takes qualities too few of us have, but which most of us can develop. We have to be quiet, to listen, to respond. We are not the initiator or the motivator; we are the reader, the recipient.

We have to be patient and wait, and wait, and wait. The suspense in the beginning of a writing course is agonizing for the teacher, but if we break first, if we do the prewriting for our students they will not learn the largest part of the writing process. *so true*

We have to respect the student, not for his product, not for the paper we call literature by giving it a grade, but for the search for truth in which he is engaged. We must listen carefully for those words that may reveal a truth, that may reveal a voice. We must respect our student for his potential truth and for his potential voice. We are coaches, encouragers, developers, creators of environments in which our students can experience the writing process for themselves.

Let us see what some of the implications of teaching process, not product are for the composition curriculum.

Implication No. 1. The text of the writing course is the student's own writing. Students examine their own evolving writing and that of their classmates, so that they study writing while it is still a matter of choice, word by word.

Implication No. 2. The student finds his own subject. It is not the job of the teacher to legislate the student's truth. It is the responsibility of the student to explore his own world with his own language, to discover his own meaning. The teacher supports but does not direct this expedition to the student's own truth.

Implication No. 3. The student uses his own language. Too often, as writer and teacher Thomas Williams points out, we teach English to our students as if it were a foreign language. Actually, most of our students have learned a great deal of language before they come to us, and they are quite willing to exploit that language if they are allowed to embark on a serious search for their own truth.

Implication No. 4. The student should have the opportunity to write all the drafts necessary for him to discover what he has to say on this particular subject. Each new draft, of course, is counted as equal to a new paper. You are not teaching a product, you are teaching a process.

Implication No. 5. The student is encouraged to attempt any form of writing which may help him discover and communicate what he has to say. The process which produces "creative" and "functional" writing is the same. You are not teaching products such as business letters and poetry, narrative and exposition. You are teaching a process your students can use—now and in the future—to produce whatever product his subject and his audience demand.

4

Implication No. 6. Mechanics come last. It is important to the writer, once he has discovered what he has to say, that nothing get between him and his reader. He must break only those traditions of written communication which would obscure his meaning.

Implication No. 7. There must be time for the writing process to take place and time for it to end. The writer must work within the stimulating tension of unpressured time to think and dream and stare out windows, and pressured time—the deadline—to which the writer must deliver.

Implication No. 8. Papers are examined to see what other choices the writer might make. The primary responsibility for seeing the choices is the student. He is learning a process. His papers are always unfinished, evolving, until the end of the marking period. A grade finishes a paper, the way publication usually does. The student writer is not graded on drafts any more than a concert pianist is judged on his practice sessions rather than on his performance. The student writer is graded on what he has produced at the end of the writing process.

Implication No. 9. The students are individuals who must explore the writing process in their own way, some fast, some slow, whatever it takes for them, within the limits of the course deadlines, to find their own way to their own truth.

Implication No. 10. There are no rules, no absolutes, just alternatives. What works one time may not another. All writing is experimental.

None of these implications require a special schedule, exotic training, extensive new materials or gadgetry, new classrooms, or an increase in federal, state, or local funds. They do not even require a reduced teaching load. What they do require is a teacher who will respect and respond to his students, not for what they have done, but for what they may do; not for what they have produced, but for what they may produce, if they are given an opportunity to see writing as a process, not a product.

5

two

Writing as Process

How Writing Finds Its Own Meaning
(1980)

At the beginning of the composing process there is only blank paper. At the end of the composing process there is a piece of writing which has detached itself from the writer and found its own meaning, a meaning the writer probably did not intend.

This process of evolving meaning—a constant revolt against intent—motivates writers. They never cease to be fascinated by what appears on their page. Writing is an act of recording or communicating and much more. Writing is a significant kind of thinking in which the symbols of language assume a purpose of their own and instruct the writer during the composing process.

This process has been revered—and feared—as a kind of magic, a process of invoking the muse, of hearing voices, of inherited talent. Many writers still think that the writing process should not be examined closely or even understood in case the magic disappear. Others of us, instructed by Janet Emig (1975), attempt to understand the relationship between the chemical and electrical interaction within the brain and the writing process. I am sympathetic to both positions, but, as a writer still trying to learn my craft at fifty-four and as a writing teacher still trying to learn how to help students learn their craft, I feel an obligation to speculate upon the writing process.

The process of making meaning with written language can not be understood by looking backward from a finished page. Process can not be inferred from product any more than a pig can be inferred from a sausage. It is possible, however, for us to follow the process forward from blank page to final draft and learn something of what happens. We can study writing as it evolves in our own minds and on our own pages and as it finds its own meaning through the hands of our writer colleagues and our writing students. We can also interview our colleagues, our students, and ourselves about what is happening when writing is happening. We can examine the testimony of writers in published interviews, such as the series of books, *Writers at Work: The Paris Review Interviews,* or in journals, letters, autobiographies, biographies, and manuscript studies. We can also consider the testimony of composers, artists, and scientists. If we attend to such available testimony, we may be able to speculate, with some authority, on how writing finds its own meaning.

But a key problem in discussing—or teaching—the writing process is that in order to analyze the process, we must give unnatural priority to one element of an explosion of elements in simultaneous action and reaction. Meaning is made through a series of almost instantaneous interactions. To study those interactions within ourselves, other writers, or our students, we must stop time (and therefore the process) and examine single elements of the writing process in unnatural isolation.

The danger is that we never recombine the elements. Some teachers present each part of the writing process to their students in a prescriptive, sequential order, creating a new kind of terrifying rhetoric which "teaches" well but "learns" poorly. It will be important for both of us—the reader and the writer—to remember throughout this chapter that we are talking about a process of interaction, not a series of logical steps. As Janet Emig has pointed out to me, we need to apply technology to our writings on process—for example, printing plastic overlays, as some textbooks do to reveal the organs of the body, as a way of showing the simultaneous interaction of the elements of writing process.

If we stand back to look at the writing process, we see the writer following the writing through the three stages of rehearsing, drafting, and revising as the piece of work—essay, story, article, poem, research paper, play, letter, scientific report, business memorandum, novel, television script moves toward its own meaning. These stages blend and overlap, but they are also distinct. Significant things happen within them. They require certain attitudes and skills on the writer's and the writing teacher's part.

The Stages of the Writing Process

The term *rehearsing*, first used by my colleague Donald Graves (1978) after observation of children writing, is far more accurate than *prewriting* to describe the activities which precede a completed draft. During this stage of the writing process the writer, in the mind and on the page, prepares himself or herself for writing before knowing for sure that there will be writing. There is a special awareness, a taking in of the writer's raw material of information, before it is clear how it will be used. When it seems there will be writing, this absorption continues, but now there is time for experiments in meaning and form, for trying out voices, for beginning the process of play which is vital to making effective meaning. The writer welcomes unexpected relationships between pieces of information from voices never before heard in the writer's head.

Drafting is the most accurate term for the central stage of the writing process, since it implies the tentative nature of our written experiments in meaning. The writer drafts a piece of writing to find out what it may have to say. The "it" is important. The writing process is a process of writing finding its own meaning. While the piece of writing is being drafted, that writing physically removes itself from the writer. Thus, it can be examined as something which may eventually stand on its own before a reader. This distancing is significant, for each draft must be an exercise in independence as well as discovery.

The final state in the writing process is *revising*. The writing stands apart from the writer, and the writer interacts with it, first to find out what the writing has to say, and then to help the writing say it clearly and gracefully. The writer moves from a broad survey of the text to line-by-line editing, all the time developing, cutting, and reordering. During this part of the process the writer must try not to force the writing to say what the writer hoped the text would say, but instead try to help the writing say what it intends to say.

One of the most important things I have learned, for example, as this piece of writing has detached itself from my intentions and instructed me, is that revision which does not end in publication becomes the most significant kind of rehearsal for the next draft. I have experienced this in my writing and observed it in my colleagues and my students. Yet I did not understand it until I found myself articulating it on these pages. I had never before seen how revising becomes rehearsal as the writer listens to the piece of writing. It may be worth noting that if you drop the *s* in the word *rehearsing*, it becomes *rehearing*. The writer *listens* to see what is on the page, scans, moves in closely, uncaps the pen, slashes sections out, moves others around, adds new ones. Somewhere along the line the writer finds that instead of looking back to the previous draft, trying to clarify what has been written, the writer is actually looking ahead to the next draft to see what must be added or cut or reordered. Revising has become rehearsing.

This process of discovering meaning—rehearsing, drafting, revising, rehearsing, drafting, revising, rehearsing—repeated again and again is the way the writing's meaning is found and made clear. This process may be seen in Figure 1.

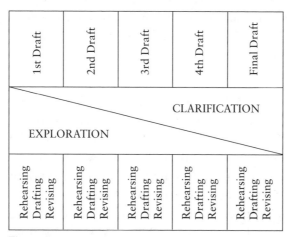

Figure 1

I had always thought of this process in rather large terms—a period of rehearsing (perhaps minutes, but more likely hours, days, weeks, months), a period of drafting (much shorter but, in the case of a book, measured in months or years), and a period of revising (which is at least as long as rehearsing). But the significant work of Sondra Perl, Director of the Writing Development Project at Lehman College, City University of New York, has made me reconsider the time in which this process works. She writes in the *New York University Education Quarterly:*

> Composing does not occur in a straightforward, linear fashion. The process is one of accumulating discrete words or phrases down on the paper and then working from these bits to reflect upon, structure, and then further develop what one means to say. It can be thought of as a kind of "retrospective structuring"; movement forward occurs only after one has reached back, which in turn occurs only after one has some sense of where one wants to go. Both aspects, the reaching back and the sensing forward, have a clarifying effect. . . . Rereading or backward movements become a way of assessing whether or not the words on the page adequately capture the original sense intended. But constructing simultaneously involves discovery. Writers know more fully what they mean only after having written it. In this way the explicit written form serves as a window on the implicit sense with which one began. (1979, 18)

Perl's work enabled me to see an instantaneous moving back and forth during the writing process. Minute by minute, perhaps second by second—or less at certain stages of the process—the writer may be rehearsing, drafting, and revising, looking back and looking forward, and acting upon what is seen and heard during the backward sensing and forward sensing.

The writer is constantly learning from the writing what it intends to say. The writer listens for evolving meaning. To learn what to do next, the writer doesn't look primarily outside the piece of writing—to rule books, rhetorical traditions, models, to previous writing experiences, to teachers or editors. To learn what to do next, the writer looks within the piece of writing. The writing itself helps to see the subject. Writing can be a lens: if the writer looks through it, he or she will see what will make the writing more effective.

The closer we move inside the writing process to speculate about how it works, the more we begin to see that what happens in the writer's mind seems much the same thing, whether the writer is rehearsing, drafting, or revising. We can document what happens during the rehearsing and revising process relatively well from the manuscript evidence and writer testimony. We can surmise from a certain authority that what happens during the drafting process is similar; but since it happens so fast, it is often imperceptible. The writer may not even be aware it is happening.

During the processes of rehearsing, drafting, and revising, four primary forces seem to interact as the writing works its way towards its own meaning. These forces are *collecting* and *connecting*, *writing* and *reading*. Writing may be ignited by any one of these forces in conjunction with any other; but once writing has begun, all of these forces begin to interact with each other. It may be helpful to look at the following diagram to see how these forces interact.

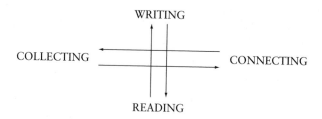

These forces interact so fast that we are often unaware of their interaction or even of their distinct existence. As we collect a piece of information, we immediately try to connect it with other pieces of information; when we write a phrase, we read it to see how it fits with what has gone before and how it may lead to what comes after. To identify these forces at work within the writing process and to understand them, we must artificially halt the interaction and examine one force at a time.

The primary forward motion of the writing process seems to come from man's unlimited hunger for *collecting* information. This need grows from the animal need for food, shelter, and safety to an intellectual need to discover meaning in experience. Man is an information-collecting organism. Information, brought to us through sight, hearing, touch, taste, smell, is stored, considered, and shared. Our education extends the range of our information-collecting through reading and research that reaches back in time and across the barriers of distance and difference.

The volume of material we gather—consciously and subconsciously—becomes so immense and is so diverse it demands *connecting*. We are compelled to provide some order for the confusion of information or it will drown us. We must discriminate, select the information that is significant, build chains of information which lead to meaning, relate immediate information to previous information, project information into the future, discover from the patterns of information what new information must be sought. The connections we make force us to see information we did not see before. The connections we are making also force us to seek new, supporting information; but, of course, some of that information doesn't support—it contradicts. So we have to make new connections with new information which in turn demands new connections. These powerful, countervailing forces work for and against each other to manufacture new meanings as we live through new experiences.

The writer fears that the collecting apparatus will be excessively controlled by the connecting apparatus. Man's dread of chaos and need for order is so fundamental that writers have to resist the desire for predictable orders, and resist the instinct to fit all new information into previously constructed meanings. The writer has to encourage the gathering of contradictory and unpredictable information which will force old meanings to adapt and new ones to be constructed.

When in good working order, these forces of collecting and connecting battle each other in a productive tension that keeps us intellectually alive, working to push back the enemies, ignorance or boredom. Neither force will give the other peace. Introduce a new piece of information and the organism immediately tries to connect it. When the organism has a connection, it seeks new information to reinforce it.

There is another pair of powerful countervailing forces at work at the same time that information is being collected and connected. The force with the primary thrust is *writing*. Man has a primitive need to write. Carol Chomsky (1971) tells us that children want to write, in fact need to write, before they want to read. And indeed someone had to write during the prelude to history; that person was also the first reader. We all have a primitive need to experience experience by articulating it. When we tell others or ourselves what has happened to us it makes that happening more real and often understandable. We need both to record and to share, both to talk to ourselves within the enormous room of the mind and to talk to others. Children—and some professors—think out loud; but for most of us, our speech is socially suppressed, done silently. Since we continue to talk to ourselves within the privacy of our skulls, some of that talking, if made public, is writing.

The act of voicing experience and connecting it involves, I think, fundamentally an aural facility. We record in written language what we say in our heads. This does not mean that writing is simply oral language written down. I believe we have a private speech we use when writing. When we know we may write, we silently practice expressing ourselves in our potential writing voices. Later we may record and revise in written language what sounded right when tried out in that silent voice within our minds. At least, this is how I think I write, dictating to myself, recording in written language what I have heard myself say milliseconds before. For many years I have dictated much of my nonfiction prose, but I was not aware until recently when I studied my own writing process that I listened to my voice while I wrote "silently" with typewriter or by pen.

Working against this powerful force of writing is the counter-force of *reading*. Put writing down on paper and it is read as it appears. Reading seems to involve criticism. We make comparisons; we look for immediate clarity, for instant grace. Just as connecting can control collecting too effectively and too early, so reading can suppress writing. The writer has to develop new forms of reading, to read loosely at first, to give the piece of writing space so that the embryonic patterns of meaning which are making shadowy appearance can have time to come clear. Writers have to learn to listen for the almost imperceptible sounds which may develop into the voice they do not expect. As the meanings come clear, the voices grow stronger. The writer has to read with increasing care, has to be critical, even surgical, but not at first.

These two forces work against each other almost simultaneously within the act of writing. In listening to the voices within our skull we "read" those voices and change them. As Perl (1979) has documented, we write and react to those marks on paper, continually testing the word against the experience, the word against the one before and the one to come next. Eventually, we extend the range of this testing to phrase, to sentence, to paragraph, to page. When I got bifocals, I had to buy lenses with an extra large reading area. They were strangely called "the executive model." But when I am writing I take them off and move my nose closer to the page. My eyes darting back and forth across my writing break out of the area bounded by my "executive" bifocals. In action writing, we do not make the separation of reading and writing that we make in school. We *writeread* or *readwrite*.

The forces of the writing process also relate to each other. This is indicated by the dotted line in the following diagram. The act of collecting is also an act of writing and reading. We cannot collect information and store it without naming it and reading that name. We also connect information by using language, whereby symbols carry the information. It is language which often seems to direct us towards significant connections, and we are led to them by the acts of writing and reading.

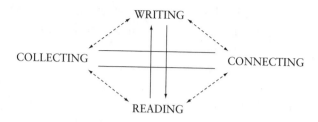

The Forces: In Balance and Out

We must always remember that each writing act is a complex instantaneous interaction. The true diagram of the writing of a sentence might look like this.

If we can manage to survive that vision after multiplying it a thousand times or more for each draft of a short essay, then we may be able to see that there is a significant sequence of balance and imbalance which takes place while the forces interact during rehearsing, drafting, and revising. During rehearsing we must give writing and collecting a slight advantage, holding off the forces of criticism and order. In revising the opposite is true. We load the dice in favor of reading and connecting. We become more critical, more orderly. The advantage holds until the balance tips. When the advantage passes again to writing and collecting, then revising becomes rehearsing.

If we see how the balance works, the scale tipped toward discovery at one time and clarification at another, then we will come to a new definition of drafting. The draft occurs when the four forces are in tentative balance. The forces have worked against each other to produce a meaning which can be read and which could perhaps be published.

In the beginning of the writing process there is no draft because the forces are wildly out of balance. The imbalance will be different with different pieces of writing, but it is there. For example, language may race ahead to the point of incoherence or be just fragmentary, a matter of notes. There may be an abundance of information which is just a jumble—no order has yet appeared from it—or there may be merely a neat, precise order, a thesis statement and outline for which there is no documentation. The process of rehearsal, however, brings the forces into balance. The writing can be read; the information begins to assume a meaningful order. The draft emerges.

The writer thinks the task is finished, that the balance will hold. But when the writer turns to read the page, it becomes apparent that the language is too stiff, too clumsy, has no flow. The reader will not follow it. Or, there is too much information; the writing goes off on tangents. Material has to be cut out and reordered. The writer may be able to help the piece of writing find its meaning through a modest amount of rewriting and researching, reordering and rereading. But many times the imbalance gets worse. The piece of writing has to follow a tangent; a new major point has to be included. Or, in fact, the major point becomes the main point. New material has to be sought out and its order discovered. The piece of writing is severely out of balance and will be brought towards balance only by rehearsing. I think it may be helpful for us to think of drafts and a series of drafts in this way, for it helps us see what has to be done to encourage a piece of writing to find its own meaning.

Continued observation and reflection upon the writing process will result in new speculations. They will come because it is our desire, reinforced by our education, to connect, to make lists, charts, maps, to find patterns and orders. This tendency is appropriate. That is what our business is. But we must remind ourselves again and again that the writing process is a kinetic activity, a matter of instantaneous motion, action and reaction which is never still. There is no clear line between the stages of rehearsing, drafting, and revising. The most meaning-producing actions may, in fact, take place on the seams between these stages when the tensions between them is the greatest.

The same thing is true of the action between the forces. We do not collect and connect and then write the connection and then read it. These forces are in action against each other, and that action produces meaning. The calm, logical moment when the words stand at dress parade and present a meaning gives no hint of the battles which produce that moment—or the battles which may be ahead.

Teaching the Composing Process

In the preceding pages I have proposed a theory of how a piece of writing finds its own meaning. That theory has come out of practice. It is rooted in the experience of making meaning with written language. Theory, however, must return to practice in our field. A writing theory that can not be practiced by teachers, writers, or students and that does not produce increasingly effective drafts of writing must be reconsidered. We also have an obligation to show how the theory can be put into practice. We must show that our students are able to write more effectively and produce pieces of writing that find their own meaning because they understand what happens during the writing act. If we accept the process theory of teaching writing, then we must be able to suggest ways in which our students can experience the writing process.

In teaching the process we have to look, not at what students need to know, but what they need to experience. This separates the teaching of writing from the teaching of a course in which the content is produced by authorities—writers of literature, scientists, historians—and interpreted by textbooks and teachers. The writing teacher has no such content. It would be bizarre for the process teacher to deliver a lecture on the process theory of composition in advance of writing—just as bizarre as it would be to deliver a lecture on rhetoric, linguistics, grammar, or any other theoretical concepts before the student writes. Such information would be meaningless to the student. It might even be harmful because the student who hears such information without the perspective of his or her own experience can develop serious misconceptions about the writing process. For example, a student might get the dangerous misconception that writers know the form before they know the content, that students know what they have to say before they say it. I would not write—would not need to write—if I knew what I was going to say before I said it. I must help my students find out through a successful writing experience why that is true.

In the writing process approach, the teacher and student face the task of making meaning together. The task is ever new, for they share the blank page and an ignorance of purpose and of outcome. They start on a trip of exploration together. They find where they are going as they get there.

This requires of the writing teacher a special kind of courage. The teacher not only has to face blank papers but blank students worried by their blankness, and a blank curriculum which worries the teacher's supervisors. The teacher has to restrain himself or herself from providing a content, taking care not to inhibit the students from finding their own subjects, their own forms, and their own language.

The writing teacher who is writing and, therefore, knows how the stages in the writing process work and how the forces within that process interact, understands the students' natural desire for premature order expressed, in part, by the question, "What do you want?" The teacher must resist the impulse to respond with a prescription. It is better to explain to the students why their writing needs room—time and space—to find its own meaning.

The first day of the writing unit should begin with writing, not talking. The students write and the teacher writes. This beginning is, of course, a symbolic gesture. It demonstrates that the information in the course will come from the student. The students produce the principal text in the writing course.

It is very hard for traditionally-trained teachers who are not writing themselves to believe that students can write without instruction from the teacher or without assignment. Teachers often do not have enough faith in their students to feel that the students

have anything to say. They also may not realize that much, perhaps most, of the poor writing they see in school is the product of
the assignments they give. Most assignments I see guarantee bad
writing. In many cases assignments direct students to write on subjects in which they have no interest and on which they have no
information. They have to adopt a point of view implicit in the
assignments or in the way teachers present them. They have to
accept forms and perhaps languages which are not appropriate to
their subjects—or their visions of the subjects.

Of course, students like assignments. Why not? They make
things easy. The good students know instantly what the teacher
wants; the poor students deliver as best they can. And neither group
has to make a personal commitment to the writing.

It is important that the writing course which is built on the
writing process set that process in action immediately. In fact, this
approach might be called the writing/response method. The student writes, then the teacher and the class respond. One device I
have used to begin a writing class is to hand out six 3 × 5 cards of
different colors. I ask the students to take a card and brainstorm
specific details about a person or place, or an event which was
important to them. They may also just brainstorm random specifics. After three or four minutes I share my own list with the class.
Then I ask them to circle a specific on their own cards which surprised them, or to connect two specifics with an unexpected relationship. I share my surprises with them. Then I tell them to take
another card and start with that moment of surprise, or just start
free writing. After three or four minutes I again share my writing
with them and ask them to take another card, to continue on, start
anew, or switch the point of view. And so we work through the
cards. At the end we each share one card, reading it aloud without
comment.

I have worked out all sorts of variations of this exercise, and so
have teachers to whom I've introduced it. The important thing is
that students write upon demand, that they write of what they
know, that they are placed under enough pressure so they write
what they did not expect to write, that the cards are small enough
and switched frequently enough so they have a new chance if one

doesn't go well, that the teacher shares his or her writing with them, that they listen to the voices which are coming from the members of their writing community, and that they discover that writing is a process of discovery.

Under such conditions I find that writing is produced. Nine hundred and ninety-nine students out of a thousand will write on demand. But if one doesn't write, not to worry. Writing is contagious. It is almost impossible to resist the desire to write in your own voice, of your own concerns, when you are part of a supportive writing community.

Sharing Writing

Once the writing is produced, it is shared. I have come to believe that this sharing, at least in the beginning, should be done orally. When students read their papers aloud they hear the voices of their classmates without the interference of mechanical problems, misspellings, and poor penmanship. Those problems will have to be dealt with in due time, but first the students—and especially the teacher—should hear the voices which come from the page.

It is equally important, perhaps more important, for the writer to hear his or her own voice. Our voices often tell us a great deal about the subject. The piece of writing speaks with its own voice of its own concerns, direction, meaning. The student writer hears that voice from the piece convey intensity, drive, energy, and more—anger, pleasure, happiness, sadness, caring, frustration, understanding, explaining. The meaning of a piece of writing comes from what it says *and* how it says it.

As the students in the writing class hear a piece of writing, they laugh with the author, grieve with the author, nod in understanding, lean forward to try to learn more. That's how the writing class begins, and that is what carries it forward. The community of writers instinctively understands that each piece of writing is trying to work its way towards a meaning. The community wants to help the writer help the piece of writing find its own meaning.

The experience of sharing writing should be reinforced by the writing conference. Individual conferences are the principal form

of instruction in the writing process approach. As we have specu-
lated upon the process by which a piece of writing finds its own
meaning, we have seen how important it is to listen to the piece of
writing and to pay attention to how that piece of writing is making
itself heard. We must, in our conferences, help the student respect
the piece of writing, pay attention to what it is trying to say, and
experience the process of helping it say it.

We get the student to talk about the paper and to talk about
the forces which produced the draft. We do this in conference, and
we do it in workshop. I have come to believe that the workshop
works best when it begins with a public conference between the
writer and the teacher. The teacher gives the student the opportunity to talk about the piece of writing—what the student sees in it,
what technical problems the student identifies, what questions the
student has for the readers—and encourages the student to talk
about the process by which the writing is being produced. The
teacher initiates the conference, but soon the class joins in, writers
helping writers listen to the evolving writing.

There are few lectures and large group exercises—if any—in
the writing class. What is there to say until a draft is heard? Who
can predict the proper response to an event which has not taken
place? There are, in fact, no classes; there are workshops in which
writing is shared. The writers in the workshop study drafts in process to see what meanings are evolving and, thereby, learn to
anticipate what may appear on the page as well as read what has
appeared.

In my own workshops I publish only the best work. The most
effective teaching occurs when the students who have produced
that work talk about how they have produced it. This is when I am
able to show students what they have learned, and by so doing I
constantly learn with them.

How were you able to get a first draft to work so well?
Well, I don't know. It just seemed to go together.
Well, what did you do before you started to write?
Not much. I didn't make an outline or anything.

Did you think much about the piece of writing you were going to do?

Oh yeah, sure. I think about it all the time, trying out different things, you know, like what you're going to say at the party, or to the girl. Stuff like that, kinda' practicing in your head.

And we're into a discussion of rehearsal as I get this student, and others, to tell about how they do this in their minds and on their pages. I underline, extend, reinforce, and teach what at least some of them have already done so that they know what they've done and may be able to apply it to other writing tasks. Others in the class who have not tried it are encouraged to try it in the future.

This is the way the writing unit unwinds. The attitudes appropriate to rehearsing, drafting, and revising are expressed in conferences and in class by the students and the teacher. The skills of rehearsing, drafting, and revising are refined after they have worked successfully on an evolving draft. Concurrently, the forces of *reading* and *writing, collecting* and *connecting* are identified. The students and the teacher share their techniques for developing and controlling these forces, for helping to bring them into effective balance.

The greatest hazard for the teacher is the natural tendency not to respect the forces and instead to supply the student with the teacher's information, to make the teacher's connection, to use the teacher's language, to read what the teacher sees in the text. The teacher must remember, in workshop and in conference, to stand back and give the student room so that the student can give the writing room to find its own meaning. The teacher should not look at the text for the student, not even with the student. The teacher looks at—and listens to—the student watching the text evolve.

The teacher is not coy and does not withhold information that the student needs. But the teacher must practice the patience and restraint of the writer. The writer treats the evolving drafts with respect, trying to help the piece of writing work towards its own meaning. The teacher demonstrates this attitude by treating the student with respect so that the student will respect his or her own evolving writing. By asking helpful questions of the student, the teacher shows the student how to question his or her own drafts: "What did you learn from this piece of writing?" "Where is the piece of writing taking you?" "What do you feel works best in this piece of writing?"

Evaluation of Writing

I am always amused when people feel that a writing course is permissive, that anything goes, that there is no serious evaluation. The fact is there is much more evaluation in the writing course than in the traditional content course. Evaluation in the writing course is not a matter of an occasional test. As the student passes through the stages of the writing process and tries to bring the forces within the process into balance, there is constant evaluation of the writing in process.

This evaluation begins with each word as it is considered and reconsidered in the mind and then as it appears on the paper. The word is reevaluated as the phrase is created and recorded. The phrase is reevaluated as the sentence is created and recorded. The sentence is reevaluated as the paragraph is created and recorded. The paragraph is reevaluated as the page is created and recorded. The page is reevaluated as the entire piece of writing is created and recorded. And then the writer, having once finished the writing and put it away, picks it up and evaluates it again.

In the writing course the writer's evaluation is shared with the teacher or with other writers in the class. The evaluation is evaluated as the writing itself is evaluated. For example:

I don't like the writing at all in this draft. It's gross.

You think it's all gross?

Yeah.

Well, I don't think it's all gross. Some of it may be gross, but what do you think is less gross?

Well, I suppose that description of how to start the snowmobile works pretty well.

Yes, that piece of writing seems to know what it's doing. Why do you think it does?

Well, it seems to be lined up pretty well. I mean, like it goes along, sort of natural.

That's how it seems to me.

Think maybe I should make the rest try to work that way? It's kind of jumbled up now.

Try it if you want.

Each draft, often each part of the draft, is discussed with read-ers—the teacher-writer and the other student-writers. Eventually the writing is published in a workshop, and a small or large group of readers evaluate it. It is evaluated on many levels. Is there a sub-ject? Does it say anything? Is it worth saying? Is it focused? Is it documented? Is it ordered? Are the parts developed? Is the writing clear? Does it have an appropriate voice? Do the sentences work? Do the paragraphs work? Are the verbs strong? Are the nouns spe-cific? Is the spelling correct? Does the punctuation clarify?

There is, in fact, so much evaluation, so much self-criticism, so much rereading, that the writing teacher has to help relieve the pressure of criticism to make sure that the writer has a bearable amount. The pressure must be there, but it never should be so great that it creates paralysis or destroys self-respect. Effective writing depends on the student's respect for the potential that may appear. The student has to have faith in the evolving draft to be able to see its value. To have faith in the draft means having faith in the self.

The teacher by the very nature of the writing course puts enor-mous pressure on the student. There are deadlines. The student will write every day. Over my desk hangs the exhortation "nulla dies sine linea," never a day without a line, which is attributed to Pliny and which has hung over Trollope's writing desk and Updike's. I give copies of it to my students, and I practice it myself. There should, in the writing unit, be at least weekly deadlines. There is an unrelenting demand for writing.

Writing means self-exposure. No matter how objective the tone or how detached the subject, the writer is exposed by words on the page. It is natural for students and for writers to fear such exposure. That fear can be relieved best if the writer, the fellow students, and the teacher look together at the piece of writing to see what the piece of writing is saying, and if they listen to the piece of writing with appropriate detachment.

When we write, we confront ourselves, but we also confront our subject. In writing the drafts of this chapter, "How Writing Finds Its Own Meaning," I found meanings I did not expect. I suppose that I was invited to do this chapter because of the definitions and the descriptions of the writing process I have published in the past. I accepted the invitation because I had completed a new description which has since been published elsewhere. But in the months that it has taken me to help this piece of writing find its own meaning I have found new meanings. This is not the chapter I intended to write. The process described here is different from what I have described before. This piece of writing revolted against my intent and taught me what I did not know.

By the time this is published I will, I hope, have moved on. There are those who may be concerned by what they consider inconsistency or disloyalty to my own words. No matter, I have no choice. The pieces of writing I have not yet thought of writing will become different from what I expect them to be when I propose them to myself. My constant is change. My teaching changes from year to year and day to day. I do not teach my students what I have learned in the past. My students teach themselves what we are learning together.

Those of us who teach the writing process are comfortable with the constant change. This sets us apart from many people in the academic world who teach in a traditional or classical mode, believing there are truths which can be learned and passed on from teacher to student, from generation to generation. Their conception has its attractions; it is the one I was taught. But my life as a writer and as a teacher of writing leads me—as similar experience has led others—to a different tradition which some call developmental or truly humanistic. We do not teach our students rules demonstrated by static models; we teach our students to write by allowing them to experience the process of writing. That is a process of discovery, of using written language to find out what we have to say. We believe this process can be adapted by our students to whatever writing tasks face them—the memo, the poem, the textbook, the speech, the consumer complaint, the job application, the story, the essay, the personal letter, the movie script, the accident report, the novel, the scientific paper. There is no way we can tell what our students will need to write in their lives beyond the classroom, but we can give our students a successful experience in the writing process. We can let them discover how writing finds its own meaning.

three

Write Before Writing
(1978)

We command our students to write and grow frustrated when our "bad" students hesitate, stare out the window, dawdle over blank paper, give up and say, "I can't write," while the "good" students smugly pass their papers in before the end of the period.

When publishing writers visit such classrooms, however, they are astonished at students who can write on command, ejaculating *EW* correct little essays without thought, for writers have to write before writing.

The writers were the students who dawdled, stared out windows, and, more often than we like to admit, didn't do well in English—or in school.

One reason may be that few teachers have ever allowed adequate time for prewriting, that essential stage in the writing process which precedes a completed first draft. And even the curricula plans and textbooks which attempt to deal with prewriting usually pass over it rather quickly referring only to the techniques of outlining, note-taking, or journal-making, not revealing the complicated process writers work through to get to the first draft.

Writing teachers, however, should give careful attention to what happens between the moment the writer receives an idea or an assignment and the moment the first completed draft is begun. We need to understand, as well as we can, the complicated and

28

intertwining processes of perception and conception through language.

In actual practice, of course, these stages overlap and interact with one another, but to understand what goes on we must separate them and look at them artificially, the way we break down any skill to study it.

First of all, we must get out of the stands where we observe the process of writing from a distance—and after the fact—and get on the field where we can understand the pressures under which the writer operates. On the field, we will discover there is one principal negative force which keeps the writer from writing and four positive forces which help the writer move forward to a completed draft.

Resistance to Writing

The negative force is *resistance* to writing, one of the great natural forces of nature. It may be called The Law of Delay: that writing which can be delayed, will be. Teachers and writers too often consider resistance to writing evil, when, in fact, it is necessary.

When I get an idea for a poem or an article or a talk or a short story, I feel myself consciously draw away from it. I seek procrastination and delay. There must be time for the seed of the idea to be nurtured in the mind. Far better writers than I have felt the same way. Over his writing desk Franz Kafka had one word, "Wait." William Wordsworth talked of the writer's "wise passiveness." Naturalist Annie Dillard recently said, "I'm waiting. I usually get my ideas in November, and I start writing in January. I'm waiting." Denise Levertov says, "If . . . somewhere in the vicinity there is a poem, then, no, I don't do anything about it, I wait."

Even the most productive writers are expert dawdlers, doers of unnecessary errands, seekers of interruptions—trials to their wives or husbands, friends, associates, and themselves. They sharpen well-pointed pencils and go out to buy more blank paper, rearrange offices, wander through libraries and bookstores, chop wood, walk, drive, make unnecessary calls, nap, daydream, and try not "consciously" to think about what they are going to write so they can think subconsciously about it.

29

Writers fear this delay, for they can name colleagues who have made a career of delay, whose great unwritten books will never be written, but, somehow, those writers who write must have the faith to sustain themselves through the necessity of delay.

Forces for Writing

In addition to that faith, writers feel four pressures that move them forward towards the first draft.

The first is *increasing information* about the subject. Once a writer decides on a subject or accepts an assignment, information about the subject seems to attach itself to the writer. The writer's perception apparatus finds significance in what the writer observes or overhears or reads or thinks or remembers. The writer becomes a magnet for specific details, insights, anecdotes, statistics, connecting thoughts, references. The subject itself seems to take hold of the writer's experience, turning everything that happens to the writer into material. And this inventory of information creates pressure that moves the writer forward toward the first draft.

Usually the writer feels an *increasing concern* for the subject. The more a writer knows about the subject, the more the writer begins to feel about the subject. The writer cares that the subject be ordered and shared. The concern, which at first is a vague interest in the writer's mind, often becomes an obsession until it is communicated. Winston Churchill said, "Writing a book was an adventure. To begin with, it was a toy and amusement; then it became a mistress, and then a master. And then a tyrant."

The writer becomes aware of a *waiting audience*, potential readers who want or need to know what the writer has to say. Writing is an act of arrogance and communication. The writer rarely writes just for himself or herself, but for others who may be informed, entertained, or persuaded by what the writer has to say.

And perhaps most important of all, is the *approaching deadline*, which moves closer day by day at a terrifying and accelerating rate. Few writers publish without deadlines, which are imposed by others or by themselves. The deadline is real, absolute, stern, and commanding.

Rehearsal for Writing

What the writer does under the pressure not to write and the four countervailing pressures to write is best described by the word _rehearsal,_ which I first heard used by Dr. Donald Graves of the University of New Hampshire to describe what he saw young children doing as they began to write. He watched them draw what they would write and heard them, as we all have, speaking aloud what they might say on the page before they wrote. If you walk through editorial offices or a newspaper city room you will see lips moving and hear expert professionals muttering and whispering to themselves as they write. Rehearsal is a normal part of the writing process, but it took a trained observer such as Dr. Graves, to identify its significance.

Rehearsal covers much more than the muttering of struggling writers. As Dr. Graves points out, productive writers are "in a state of rehearsal all the time." Rehearsal usually begins with an unwritten dialogue within the writer's mind. "All of a sudden I discover what I have been thinking about a play," says Edward Albee. "This is usually between six months and a year before I actually sit down and begin typing it out." The writer thinks about characters or arguments, about plot or structure, about words and lines. The writer usually hears something which is similar to what Wallace Stevens must have heard as he walked through his insurance office working out poems in his head.

What the writer hears in his or her head usually evolves into note-taking. This may be simple brainstorming, the jotting down of random bits of information which may connect themselves into a pattern later on, or it may be journal-writing, a written dialogue between the writer and the subject. It may even become research recorded in a formal structure of note-taking.

Sometimes the writer not only talks to himself or herself, but to others—collaborators, editors, teachers, friends—working out the piece of writing in oral language with someone else who can enter into the process of discovery with the writer.

For most writers, the informal notes turn into lists, outlines, titles, leads, ordered fragments, all sketches of what later may be written, devices to catch a possible order that exists in the chaos of the subject.

In the final stage of rehearsal, the writer produces test drafts, written or unwritten. Sometimes they are called discovery drafts or trial runs or false starts that the writer doesn't think will be false. All writing is experimental, and the writer must come to the point where drafts are attempted in the writer's head and on paper.

Some writers seem to work more in their head, and others more on paper. Susan Sowers, a researcher at the University of New Hampshire, examining the writing processes of a group of graduate students found

> a division . . . between those who make most discoveries during prewriting and those who make most discoveries during writing and revision. The discoveries include the whole range from insights into personal issues to task-related organizational and content insight. The earlier the stage at which insights occur, the greater the drudgery associated with the writing-rewriting tasks. It may be that we resemble the young reflective and reactive writers. The less developmentally mature reactive writers enjoy writing more than reflective writers. They may use writing as a rehearsal for thinking just as young, reactive writers draw to rehearse writing. The younger and older reflective writers do not need to rehearse by drawing to write or by writing to think clearly or to discover new relationships and significant content.

This concept deserves more investigation. We need to know about both the reflective and reactive prewriting mode. We need to see if there are developmental changes in students, if they move from one mode to another as they mature, and we need to see if one mode is more important in certain writing tasks than others. We must, in every way possible, explore the significant writing stage of rehearsal which has rarely been described in the literature on the writing process.

The Signals Which Say "Write"

During the rehearsal process, the experienced writer sees signals which tell the writer how to control the subject and produce a working first draft. The writer, Rebecca Rule, points out that in some cases when the subject is found, the way to deal with it is inherent in the subject. The subject itself is the signal. Most writers have experienced this quick passing through of the prewriting process. The line is given and the poem is clear; a character gets up and walks the writer through the story; the newspaperman attends a press conference, hears a quote, sees the lead and the entire structure of the article instantly. But many times the process is far less clear. The writer is assigned a subject or chooses one and then is lost.

E. B. White testifies, "I never knew in the morning how the day was going to develop. I was like a hunter hoping to catch sight of a rabbit." Denise Levertov says, "You can smell the poem before you see it." Most writers know these feelings but students who have never seen a rabbit dart across their writing desks or smelled a poem need to know the signals which tell them that a piece of writing is near.

What does the writer recognize which gives a sense of closure, a way of handling a diffuse and overwhelming subject? There seem to be eight principal signals to which writers respond.

One signal is *genre*. Most writers view the world as a fiction writer, a reporter, a poet, or an historian. The writer sees experience as a plot or a lyric poem or a news story or a chronicle. The writer uses such literary traditions to see and understand life.

"Ideas come to a writer because he has trained his mind to seek them out," says Brian Garfield. "Thus when he observes or reads or is exposed to a character or event, his mind sees the story possibilities in it and he begins to compose a dramatic structure in his mind. This process is incessant. Now and then it leads to something that will become a novel. But it's mainly an attitude: a way of looking at things; a habit of examining everything one perceives as potential material for a story."

Genre is a powerful but dangerous lens. It both clarifies and limits. The writer and the student must be careful not to see life merely in the stereotype form with which he or she is most familiar but to look at life with all of the possibilities of the genre in mind and to attempt to look at life through different genre.

Another signal the writer looks for is a *point of view.* This can be an opinion towards the subject or a position from which the writer—and the reader—studies the subject.

A tenement fire could inspire the writer to speak out against tenements, dangerous space-heating system, a fire-department budget cut. The fire might also be seen from the point of view of the people who were the victims or who escaped or who came home to find their home gone. It may be told from the point of view of a fireman, an arsonist, an insurance investigator, a fire-safety engineer, a real-estate planner, a housing inspector, a landlord, a spectator, as well as the victim. The list could go on.

Still another way the writer sees the subject is through *voice.* As the writer rehearses, in the writer's head and on paper, the writer listens to the sound of the language as a clue to the meaning of the subject and the writer's attitude toward that meaning. Voice is often the force which drives a piece of writing forward, which illuminates the subject for the writer and the reader.

A writer may, for example, start to write a test draft with detached unconcern and find that the language appearing on the page reveals anger or passionate concern. The writer who starts to write a solemn report of a meeting may hear a smile and then a laugh in his own words and go on to produce a humorous column.

News is an important signal for many writers who ask what the reader needs to know or would like to know. Those prolific authors of nature books, Lorus and Margery Milne, organize their books and each chapter in the books around what is new in the field. Between assignment and draft they are constantly looking for the latest news they can pass along to their readers. When they find what is new, then they know how to organize their writing.

Writers constantly wait for the *line* which is given. For most writers, there is an enormous difference between a thesis or an idea or a concept and an actual line, for the line itself has resonance. A single line can imply a voice, a tone, a pace, a whole way of treating a subject. Joseph Heller tells about the signal which produced his novel *Something Happened*.

I begin with a first sentence that is independent of any conscious preparation. Most often nothing comes out of it: a sentence will come to mind that doesn't lead to a second sentence. Sometimes it will lead to thirty sentences which then come to a dead end. I was alone on the deck. As I sat there worrying and wondering what to do, one of those first lines suddenly came to mind: "In the office in which I work, there are four people of whom I am afraid. Each of these four people is afraid of five people." Immediately, the lines presented a whole explosion of possibilities and choices—characters (working in a corporation), a tone, a mood of anxiety, or of insecurity. In that first hour (before someone came along and asked me to go to the beach) I knew the beginning, the ending, most of the middle, the whole scene of that particular "something" that was going to happen; I knew about the brain-damaged child, and especially, of course, about Bob Slocum, my protagonist, and what frightened him, that he wanted to be liked, that his immediate hope was to be allowed to make a three-minute speech at the company convention. Many of the actual lines throughout the book came to me—the entire "something happened" scene with those solar plexus lines (beginning with the doctor's statement and ending with "Don't tell my wife" and the rest of them) all coming to me in the first hour on that Fire Island deck. Eventually I found a different opening chapter with a different first line ("I get the willies when I see closed doors") but I kept the original which had spurred everything to start off the second section. (in Plimpton 1974)

Newspapermen are able to write quickly and effectively under pressure because they become skillful at identifying a lead, that first line—or two or three—which will inform and entice the reader and which, of course, also gives the writer control over the subject. As an editorial writer, I found that finding the title first gave me control over the subject. Each title became, in effect, a pre-draft, so that in listing potential titles I would come to one which would be a signal as to how the whole editorial could be written.

Poets and fiction writers often receive their signals in terms of an *image*. Sometimes this image is static; other times it is a moving picture in the writer's mind. When Gabriel García Marquez was asked what the starting point of his novels was, he answered, "A completely visual image . . . the starting point of *Leaf Storm* is an old man taking his grandson to a funeral, in *No One Writes to the Colonel,* it's an old man waiting, and in *One Hundred Years,* an old man taking his grandson to the fair to find out what ice is." William Faulkner was quoted as saying, "It begins with a character, usually, and once he stands up on his feet and begins to move, all I do is trot along behind him with a paper and pencil trying to keep up long enough to put down what he says and does." It's a comment which seems facetious—if you're not a fiction writer. Joyce Carol Oates adds, "I visualize the characters completely; I have heard their dialogue, I know how they speak, what they want, who they are, nearly everything about them."

Although image has been testified to mostly by imaginative writers, where it is obviously most appropriate, I think research would show that nonfiction writers often see an image as the signal. The person, for example, writing a memo about a manufacturing procedure may see the assembly line in his or her mind. The politician arguing for a pension law may see a person robbed of a pension, and by seeing that person know how to organize a speech or the draft of a new law.

Many writers know they are ready to write when they see a *pattern* in a subject. This pattern is usually quite different from what we think of as an outline, which is linear and goes from beginning to end. Usually the writer sees something which might be called a gestalt, which is, in the world of the dictionary, "a unified physical, psychological, or symbolic configuration having properties that cannot be derived from its parts." The writer usually in a moment sees the entire piece of writing as a shape, a form, something that is more than all of its parts, something that is entire and is represented in his or her mind, and probably on paper, by a shape.

Marge Piercy says, "I think that the beginning of fiction, of the story, has to do with the perception of pattern in event." Leonard Gardner, in talking of his fine novel *Fat City,* said, "I had a definite design in mind. I had a sense of circle . . . of closing the circle at the end." John Updike says, "I really begin with some kind of solid, coherent image, some notion of the shape of the book and even of its texture. *The Poorhouse Fair* was meant to have a sort of wide shape. *Rabbit, Run* was kind of zigzag. *The Centaur* was sort of a sandwich."

We have interviews with imaginative writers about the writing process, but rarely interviews with science writers, business writers, political writers, journalists, ghost writers, legal writers, medical writers—examples of effective writers who use language to inform and persuade. I am convinced that such research would reveal that they also see patterns or gestalts which carry them from idea to draft.

"It's not the answer that enlightens but the question," says Ionesco. This insight into what the writer is looking for is one of the most significant considerations in trying to understand the freewriting process. A most significant book based on more than ten years of study of art students, *The Creative Vision: A Longitudinal Study of Problem-Finding in Art,* by Jacob W. Getzels and Mihaly Csikszentmihalyi (1976), has documented how the most creative students are those who come up with the *problem* to be solved rather than a quick answer. The signal to the creative person may well be the problem, which will be solved through the writing.

We need to take all the concepts of invention from classical rhetoric and combine them with what we know from modern psychology, from studies of creativity, from writers' testimony about the prewriting process. Most of all, we need to observe successful students and writers during the prewriting process, and to debrief them to find out what they do when they move effectively from assignment or idea to completed first draft. Most of all, we need to move from failure-centered research to research which defines what happens when the writing goes well, just what is the process followed by effective student and professional writers. We know far too little about the writing process.

Implications for Teaching Writing

Our speculations make it clear that there are significant implications for the teaching of writing in a close examination of what happens between receiving an assignment or finding a subject and beginning a completed first draft. We may need, for example, to reconsider our attitude toward those who delay writing. We may, in fact, need to force many of our glib, hair-trigger student writers to slow down, to daydream, to waste time, but not to avoid a reasonable deadline.

We certainly should allow time within the curriculum for prewriting, and we should work with our students to help them understand the process of rehearsal, to allow them the experience of rehearsing what they will write in their minds, on the paper, and with collaborators.

We should also make our students familiar with the signals they may see during the rehearsal process which will tell them that they are ready to write, that they have a way of dealing with their subject.

The prewriting process is largely invisible; it takes place within the writer's head or on scraps of paper that are rarely published. But we must understand that such a process takes place, that it is significant, and that it can be made clear to our students. Students who are not writing, or not writing well, may have a second chance if they are able to experience the writers' counsel to write before writing.

four

The Daybook

My principal work is seeing by seeing/seeing by writing/
the daybook is my main work—my lab—my publication
will be what is reported out of my lab.

*The daybook was one of Don's most important writing tools.
Here in an essay he explains why and how he uses his daybook. We have included pages from one of the books that
show Don thinking about writing and teaching. These pages
also include a plan—one of hundreds Don drew up over the
years—for getting writing done; a list of what he was doing
and should be doing each morning; and some of Don's drawings. (Don believed others would benefit from creating their
own daybooks, but he never wanted anyone to copy what he
did; he believed each writer should make the daybook exactly
what she needed it to be.) In these pages he wrote, "The
important thing is the act of seeing. There must be joy in the
act of writing or I shall not write—delight (a child's delight)
in the placing of marks on paper."*

The most valuable writing tool I have is my daybook, and the
name is important to me. For years I tried to keep a journal. I imagined
I was Gide or Camus. I wasn't, and what I wrote was not perceptive, but
pompous, full of hot air, hilarious to read, and utterly useless to me as
a writer. At other times I tried to keep a diary or a log, but then I
found myself recording trivia, the temperature, or who I met, or what I
ate. It made a rather boring life seem even more boring.

I don't know where I heard the term daybook, but a number of
years ago I found myself using the term and writing every day - well,
almost every day - in a 10 x 8 spiral notebook filled with greenish paper,
narrow ruled, and with a margin line down the left. This worked for me.
I write in my lap, in the living room or on the porch, in the car or an
airplane, in meetings at the university, in bed, or stopping while I walk
and sitting down on a rock wall. A bound book doesn't work for me. I find
a spiral book much more convenient, and since I write in all sorts of
light, indoors and out, I find the greenish paper comfortable. I chose
the size because it fits in the outside pocket of the canvas bag I have
with me all the time.

The organization is simple day-by-day chronology. When I change
the subject I make a code word in the margine. That way I can look back
through the book and collect all the notes I've made on a single project
or concern.

I usually write in the daybook the first fifteen minutes of the
day before I eat breakfast. And then I have it near me all day long. If
something occurs to me I make a note during a television commercial or in
a meeting, or while walking, or in the car.

How I use my daybook varies from time to time. But it is always a form of talking to myself, a way of thinking on paper. And some of my writing that seems spontaneous has left tracks through years of daybooks.

If you look through my daybook here are some of the things you would see:

. Questions that need to be answered.

. Fragments of writing seeking a voice.

. Leads, hundreds of leads.

. Titles, hundreds of titles.

. Notes from which I have made lectures, talks, or speeches.

. Notes I have made at lectures, talks, or speeches. Also notes I have made at poetry readings, hockey games, and concerts.

. Outlines.

. Ideas for stories, articles, poems, books, papers.

. Diagrams showing how a piece might be organized or, more likely, showing the relationships between parts of an idea.

. Drafts.

. Observations.

. Quotations from writers or artists.

. Newspaper clippings.

. Titles of books to be read.

. Notes on reading.

. Pictures I've pasted in.

. Writing schedules.

. Pasted in copies of letters I've written and want to save.

. Lists, lots of lists.

. Pasted in handouts I've developed for classes or workshops.

T here's no way I have to use the daybook. Anything that will stimulate or record my thinking, anything that will move me towards writing goes into the daybook. When a notebook is filled I go through and harvest a page or two or three of the most interesting material for the beginning of the next daybook. When I'm ready to work seriously on a project I go back through the daybooks for a year or more and photocopy those pages that relate to the subject I'm working on.

The daybook stimulates my thinking, helps me make use of those small fragments of time which is all the time we have on many days to write. It keeps my writing muscles in condition; it lets me know what I'm concerned with making into writing; it increases my productivity. In every way it is a helpful habit.

If you decide to keep a daybook make it your own. Don't try to follow anyone else's formula. And don't write it for another audience. It's a private place where you can think and where you can be dumb, stupid, sloppy, silly; where you can do all the bad writing and bad thinking that are essential for those few moments of insight that produce good writing.

WRITING PLANS - 2ND HALF 1988

- WRITE NOVEL + GLOBE + POETRY
- Prepare SHOPTALK + HANDBOOK

#	DATE	MON	TUE	WED	THU	FRI	SAT	SUN	GLOBE	Other Writing
1	7/4		•							PLAN NOVEL
2	11								C	↓
3	18		•	UNH						NOVEL 1
4	25	UNH	,	GLOBE					C	1,000 WORDS 2
5	8/1									FIVE DAY A WEEK
6	8								C	3
7	15		•							4
8	22								C	
9	29								N	
10	9/5			GLOBE					C	5
11	12		•							6
12	19								C	7
13	26		•	GLOBE					N	8
14	10/3					UNH	→		C	9
15	10									
16	17								C	
17	24								N	
18	31			GLOBE					C	10
19	11/7		•							11
20	14								C	12
21	21		•		THANK					13
22	28			GLOBE					C	14
23	12/5	• ROX BOSTON								15
24	12								C	
25	19									
26	26								C	

43

Daybook   **August 12, 2000**

<u>Assumptions</u>

   . I need to write every day for my mental and emotion health.
   . I need to exercise every day for my physical health.
   . I cannot count on writing or doing office work in the afternoon
     or evening.

<u>What I Do In The Morning</u>	<u>What I Should Do In The Morning</u>
. Get up at 5:30	Get up at 5:00
	Walk 30 minutes
. Coffee with Bob and Michael	OK
. Eat Breakfast	OK
[Some days late with MM]	Only on weekends
. Read the Globe and the Times	Before supper
. Nap?	Only if necessary, then only for ten
	minutes.
. Go to office before 8:00	OK
. Read and answer e-mail	After writing
. Write	OK
	Make on sketch after writing.
. Make and accept telephone calls	After writing
. File only when necessary	Each morning after writing
. Rarely write snail mail	Each morning after writing

Writing

SHOULD BE AN ART

WRITING IS AN ACT OF SEEING

↓

WRITING IS ACTIVE

THERE SHOULD BE DELIGHT - JOY - SATISFACTION IN THE ACT OF
putting words on paper.

IN THE TOOLS — PEN - INK - PAPER
IN SEEING WHAT IS MADE
IN making AND seeing WHAT IS MADE.

YOU WRITE IN A JOURNAL. TO RECORD

(DISCOVER WHAT YOU ARE SEEING;
WHAT YOU ARE KNOWING)

. TO REFLECT, RECONSIDER

. TO CONNECT

THE JOURNAL IS A MAP OF THE MIND A COUNTRY
which IS EVER CHANGING —

IT WOULD BE NO. FUN TO MAP
A COUNTRY WHICH COULD BE MAPPED

THIS DAYBOOK will BE AN ARTIST'S SKETCHBOOK —

A WORKING BOOK, A SOURCE BOOK
IT will BE worked in EACH DAY IN SPARE
moments — THEN MINED LATER.

IT WILL INCLUDE:

- THE NOVEL
- POEMS
- ARTICLES AND PAPERS FOR THE NON-FICTION BOOK
- LAB NOTES ON THE WRITING PROCESS
- QUOTES FOR THE FILE
- NOTES ON THE STUDY OF DRAWING
- SKETCHES

THE IMPORTANT THING IS THE
ACT OF SEEING
UNDERSTANDING
OF UNDERSTANDING
THROUGH THE ACT
OF PLACING LINES
WHICH MAY BE
WORDS ON THE
PAGE

I SHALL PUT INFORMATION ON THE PAGE AND EDGE
PIECES OF IT CLOSER ENOUGH TOGETHER SO IT WILL
GIVE OFF MEANING

WRITING IS CALLIGRAPHY

    THE MAKING OF MARKS IN THE DESK

                  IN STONE

                  IN WOOD

                  ON PAPER

A WORD IS A PICTURE OF AN IDEA

A WORD IS A DRAWING OF WHAT CAN'T BE SEEN

———

MY PRINCIPAL WORK IS SEEING BY SEEING

                SEEING BY WRITING

    THE DAYBOOK IS MY MAIN WORK — MY LAB —

    MY PUBLICATION WILL BE WHAT IS REPORTED

    OUT OF MY LAB

———

THERE MUST BE JOY IN THE ACT OF WRITING OR I

SHALL NOT WRITE — DELIGHT (A CHILD'S DELIGHT)

IN THE PLACING OF MARKS ON PAPER.

———

IN DEBT TO WALLACE STEVENS ⟶ "The tongue is an eye"

THE PEN IS AN EYE

THE PEN IS AN EAR

THE PEN IS A TONGUE

P
E   PEN   PEN
N

N
E
P

P E N

THE PEN IS MY FACE

MY PEN SHOWS ME

WHO I AM

PEN A BLACK FINGER

PEN A FOOT

WYETH ON TODAY SHOW THIS MORNING:

SKETCHING LIKE FENCING

I AM A FOLLOWER OF THE PEN

(LANGUAGE LEADS I FOLLOW)

THE PEN LEADS, I FOLLOW

SOME PENS I SHALL FOLLOW:

PEN - MONT BLANC #24 FINE POINT

PEN - MONT BLANC #220 EXTRA FINE POINT

PEN - STYLIST

PEN - ALL-LITE STAINLESS STEEL
                  EX. FINE POINT

PEN - FLAIR

PEN - BIC ACCOUNTANT FINE PT. AF-49

PEN - UNI

PEN - PILOT

PEN - FLAIR (GRAY)

WHAT I NEED IS A

ZOOM PEN

WHICH GOES FROM BROAD TO

EXTRA FINE

I will keep this daybook with me and use it whenever I can find a moment for observation, exploration or reflection. This should make productive use of fragments of time during a busy schedule. When I have more time, I will write from this notebook.

<u>SABBATICAL BOOK (s)</u> ?

1) ON <u>WRITING</u>

2) ON <u>TEACHING</u> <u>WRITING</u>

PUT ARTICLES, QUOTES, TALKS AND NOTES
INTO CHAPTER NOTEBOOKS

DO WE DISCOVER BY WRITING

OR DOES WRITING MAKE OUR
DISCOVERIES VISIBLE

IT MUST BE FUN TO <u>MAKE</u> THIS CONTINUAL,
DAILY BOOK. TONIGHT I HAVE
REDISCOVERED SOMETHING OF THE
WONDER OF WRITING —
BACK TO BASICS
(DREW)

HUDSON – POST ARTICLE
STUDENTS – REQ.

I'M PROUD TO BE A TEACHER (GLAD I DON'T HAVE HIGH SCHOOL LOAD)
UNEDUCATED AS A TEACHER
BUT, I'M A WRITER FIRST

  I TEACH WHAT I'VE LEARNED AT MY TRADE +
  WHAT I RELEARN EVERY DAY –
    QUESTIONS YOU'D LIKE TO ASK A WRITER
    NOTES ON WHAT A WRITER DOES

IF YOU WERE TO <u>IMAGINE</u> A WRITER

   YOUNG - STRONG PROFILE
    LONG HAIR, THIN WAIST
    LIMP WRIST
    EFFEMINATE ?
   SENSITIVE - OTHER WORLDY
    AESTHETIC
    NERVOUS - HIGH STRUNG
    CYNICAL
  TALENTED - A GIFT
    INSPIRATION, MAGIC
    REPORTER OF VISIONS
     PEN SCUTTLING AHEAD OF IDEAS
  STARVING OR RICH
  GLAMOR - PUBLICATION PARTIES
    A GAY ROUND
    WITTY CONVERSATION
    WOMEN - OR MEN - FRIENDS

THIS ROMANTIC NOTION OF WRITER IS RIDICULOUS –

  WOULD BE UNIMPORTANT EXCEPT FOR

  THE FACT IT HAS INFLUENCED

  TEACHING OF WRITING AND

  THE STANDARDS OF WRITING MAINTAINED
   IN EVERY DEPARTMENT

ALLOW me to DISPELL SUCH ILLUSIONS

WHAT DOES THIS TRUE PICTURE OF WRITER MEAN TO YOU

    ALL TEACHERS OF WRITING

    PUBLISH OR PERISH –

        WRITING CHEAPEST, TOUGHEST, BEST TEST

YOU SHOULD DEMAND GOOD WRITING.
    TEACH STUDENTS TO SEE, THINK ABOUT WHAT THEY'VE SEEN
    INSIST ON CLARITY
            → SPECIFICS NOT generalization – BRESLIN
      INDIVIDUAL IDEAS – THOUGHT, CONTENT
             NOT WORDS, IDEAS FIRST – ENGLISH TEACHERS
      ORDER (– OUTLINE)   FRESHMAN ENGLISH

      SHORT PIECES – HARDER TO WRITE SHORT
          DON'T GRADE ON LENGTH, WEIGHT, BINDERS
      REWRITE
        REWRITE | DEFINITIONS
         REWRITE | IMPORTANT SUBJECT MATTER

      NOT FEW WITH TALENT – MOST COLLEGE BOUND
           (+ OTHERS TALENT)
       TALENT CHEAP, COMMON – CAN'T BE BRUISED
         TALENT IS TOUGH
        HARD WORK
     GIVE STUDENTS SATISFACTION OF TOUGH JOB
        OF EXPRESSING THEMSELVES

        SAYING SOMETHING OF THEIR OWN
        WORTH SAYING

        CLEARLY, SIMPLY, STRONGLY
         ACCURATELY, WITH PRECISION OF MIND
           AND WORD

WRITING IS DIFFICULT, WORTHWHILE

      AS HARD AS MATH, AS ELEGANT AS SCIENCE, AS
      EFFICIENT AS A GOOD ENGINE, AS LOGICAL AS PHILOSOPHY
      VEHICLE BY WHICH MOST IMPORTANT IDEAS ARE RECORDED, PASSED ON
OH YES, IT'S HARD TO TEACH

      MINDS OF OUR STUDENTS NEED WHETSTONE OF OUR MINDS
      FRIGHTENING WHEN WE HAVE WHEELS OF CHEESE
MY EXPERIENCE RESPOND TO HARD WORK

<u>HOW WRITER DISCOVERS</u>

- BY WRITING, NOT THINKING ABOUT WRITING
  (WRITING THIS - VI. TEACHERS OF ENGLISH)
- OUT OF NEED - ORDER + SHAPE LIFE
    1) EXPLORATION - DISCOVERY (ONLY ONE THEME?)
    2) COMMUNICATION

- STIMULUS - PUTS HIMSELF IN WAY OF EXPERIENCE
    - AWARENESS
    - CURIOSITY → EXTERNAL
    - RESPONSE - SELF-CENTEREDNESS - INTERNAL
        "MUSEUM"

    NEED AN ABUNDANCE OF INFORMATION

- FORM - DISCOVERED FORM - GRAPHIC FORM
    - ACT OF FAITH
    - AID to MEANING - NEWSTORY
                      - STORY
                      - ARGUEMENT

- EMPTINESS - STARING OUT WINDOW - TAPPING SUBCONCIOUS
    "MY FIRST DYING"

- MAKING CONNECTIONS
    BRAINSTORMING - IDEA TECHNIQUE
    WRITING to BE RIDICULOUS

- TONE - VOICE

- POINT OF VIEW - TOWARDS SUBJECT
                - WITHIN SUBJECT

- WORD CHOICE

HOW WRITER DISCOVERS (2)

- WRITER'S memory
  memory BY writing

- DISCOVERS through sharing
  with other writers
  more by community THAN writer/writers

- DISCOVERS through other arts
  Film
  Music
  ART - "MUSEUM"

- DISCOVERS by being DISLOYAL
  SKEPTICAL - questioning

- Being open to DIFFERENCE, CHANGE

- JOURNAL / NOTES

Implications for teaching:

- Open - Teaching A
  Demonstration of
  This

- Create A Climate
  Failure possible
  Discovery a goal

- Discovers by being honest
  1st about himself
  Amused at own response to common
  question

five

Listening to Writing
(1980)

In trying to write an essay which would speculate about how the writer discovers the draft which marks the watershed between pre-writing and rewriting, I heard a poem. And in hearing the poem I found this essay which made me newly aware of the importance of listening to writing—both as a writer and a teacher of writing.

A poem was unexpected. As much as I welcome the surprises which are central to the writing process, I felt a bit guilty. Poetry was not on the agenda. I had just finished a draft of a novel and was beginning to revise it. That had first priority. I had this article to do, and it was fighting the novel for first priority as the deadline approached. I had a busy schedule of teaching, traveling, and talking this spring. There was no time for poetry. But on a Saturday, when I had a clear day at home, a day when I had programmed myself to split the morning between editing the novel and drafting this essay, I spent the morning on a poem. When a poem comes, I listen. I have to remind myself that the purpose of my writing routine is to make me receptive to writing—the writing that wants to make its voice heard. That is not always the writing which is expected but I must seize the gift and toss aside the schedule.

It is my habit to begin the day grinding coffee and putting the kettle on the stove. When the pot boils I sit down and twist the dial of a pocket timer to fifteen minutes. I open a 10-by-8-inch narrow-ruled spiral notebook (National 33-008) with green eye-ease paper on my beanbag lap-desk, and uncap my pen (Esprit DLX with black ink and 0.5mm superfine point).

The tools are important. Most craftsmen are compulsive about their tools, and writers work with pen, pencil, typewriter and paper which are familiar to hand and eye. Secretly, I think most writers believe the writing is either in the page or the pen, somehow magically released by the act of writing.

Time is also important. I try to start each day with a few quiet moments when I listen for writing, listen to hear the words I watch my pen put on the page. I may hear—and capture—drafts, titles, lines, leads, details, lists, ideas, memories, scenes, notes for stories, textbooks, reportage, profiles, essays, poems, plays; whatever comes to my ear is captured on the page. The quiet moments when this happens have a religious quality for me. This quiet time is made possible by habit. I do not get up eager to write. I do not get up even eager to get up. But it is my habit to turn on the timer, open the notebook, uncap the pen, and listen.

Writing usually comes—100 words, 5, 152, 18, 249. No matter. I am simply waiting, listening. If no words arrive at my ear I may think back to a moment of intense feeling—when I was eight and found Grandmother collapsed on the stairs or the moment in combat when I knew I could kill. Or I may brainstorm, catching the specific and apparently unrelated fragments—images, words, details—which pass through our minds as we meditate. I may describe the plant on the table across the room or the scene in the corridor outside the classroom yesterday, because description best ignites writing. I may also play with words. For example, in thinking about my mother's militant Christianity I was interested when I heard two words collide: angry prayers. Those words may give off a poem, a story, an essay, or flicker out and die. It does not matter, at this time, what—if anything—is produced.

If no words come that is fine. I suppress the panic I feel at silence. There will be another day; the writing will come if I wait, and I often do have to wait minutes which seem like hours. My students tell me after they write in class that they had to wait ten minutes, fifteen minutes, half an hour before they could get going. I have timed their long periods of waiting; it seems a long time to them, but it is often only 30 seconds, 105 seconds, 90 seconds, sometimes even 120 seconds. We are educated for busyness, not educated for listening to our own minds at work. I worry more, in fact, when my words come too easily. It is important that I discipline myself to sit down and be quiet, but I am not an assembly line, I do not have to produce. The irony, of course, is that the more peaceful I am, the more quietly receptive, the less I drive myself to produce, the more productive I become.

I try to come to my 15-minute appointment with the blank page as empty of conscious intent as possible. I want no internal noise—the carping of the critic at my last piece, the echoes of past failure or past success, the sandbox bickering of campus politics, the endless listing of what isn't done and must be done—to interfere with what I may hear. External noise does not bother me and I usually write in the morning with the television news or a classical FM music program in the background, but the internal noise of my own busyness can create so much noise I cannot hear my own voice and therefore cannot write.

Of course, I do not really come emptyheaded to any morning's writing. When I am most clear of intention my life lies raw and open to my pen. The other evening, at a poetry reading by Heather McHugh, my notebook was open, my pen uncapped. The better the poetry reading, the more likely that unexpected lines of poetry will arrive. I was ready for the line that rose from within myself: "The dead swim in the earth." The next morning these four lines slowly arranged themselves on the page:

> the father who has buried his daughter
> knows the dead swim in the earth
> whales shapes of memory rising
> to make him stagger as he walks

I have to listen to my autobiography, no matter how painful it is. I must hear the writing which demands to speak.

Every writer—student or professional—comes to the page with a personal history as a human being and as a writer; I am well aware of how my autobiography brought me, on that Sunday morning, to the poem which is central to this essay. I have been a writer since I published a fourth-grade newspaper by hectograph. I have wanted to be a drawer and a painter, and still do. I have long been concerned about the making of art. New poetry usually arrives in bunches, like a car full of uninvited relatives.

Three other forces had impelled me towards a poem. I had made notes on a plane flying home from Charlotte, North Carolina, playing with the idea of a book of poetry called, "An Essay on the Line," which would tell the important things about lines, dots, curves, squares, and triangles my high school geometry book left out. I had had lunch two days before with a fine artist on our faculty, John Hatch, who had talked about how a painting talks to him while he is living within the act of painting. He had given me a marvelous quotation by Cennino Cennini on how the artist discovers "things not seen, hiding themselves under the shadow of natural objects." The mail brought me word that several poems had been accepted and, like my students, I am motivated more by acceptance than rejection. So, on Sunday morning, I found my pen putting down:

AN ESSAY ON THE LINE
THE LINE
THE LINE COMES FROM WHAT THE HAND
DIDN'T KNOW IT KNEW
    LINE
THE TELLS THE HAND WHAT IT KNEW

THE LINE IS (RECOGNIZED) NAMED
IT IS A HAND
REACHING

LINES MAKE CONNECTIONS
OF THEIR OWN
IF THE HAND THAT IS DRAWING THEM
~~SEES~~
FINDS THEM

THIS LINE IS A ROCK
THAT A STONE

S IS A TREE
THE LINE CRACKS THE STONE
IT

BUT THE TREE IS NOT THAT TREE
OVER THERE
THE STONE
THE ONE ONCE SEEN

IT IS THE STONE
ON THE PAGE
WITH ITS OWN HISTORY
OF FROST AND WARM
THE INSIDIOUS WATER
THE ICE
THE TREE WHICH HAS BECOME
A PART OF IT

ON THIS PAGE
IT IS NOT A STONE
SPLIT BY A TREE
OR A TREE SPLITTING
A STONE

IT IS A STONE TREE
A TREE STONE

MADE BY ONE BY THEIR
NOT: SHAPED HISTORY

THE PAGE FLUTTERS   (MOVE EARLIER?)
TO THE GROUND

THIS TREE   ROCK
SPLITTING THIS PAGE
IS TOO REAL A TREE
TO BE TRUE

THE HAND MOVES A ROCK
WHICH HAS BEEN
SPLIT BY A TREE
A ROCK OF HALVES
~~NOT KNEW~~
NO LONGER KNOWING EACH OTHER

THE HAND
TEARS UP THE PAGE

That was fifteen minutes' writing, perhaps a bit more self-conscious than normal because it was a poem about art. I was aware of how didactic the first lines were, but I suppressed the critic and did not worry at this time about how unpoetic most of the other lines were. I have to listen to the writing and nothing else. I have to try and hear the soft but true voice hidden under the loud but clumsy voice in an early draft. I have learned that writing evolving often stumbles, but what seem to be mistakes often turn out to be keys to meaning.

I was surprised and excited when one line made a rock and another line a tree. I had no idea that would happen, but when it did, I had something that was real in my mind's eye. I could study the rock and the tree to see what they meant. I felt then the poem might grow into a piece of writing, not a statement about writing. There was no calculation which produced that rock, that tree; they weren't pre-thought. This is not automatic writing in the sense it is dictated from a spirit world, and it is not an un-intellectual act. It is both intensely intellectual and intensely emotional as language brings thought, feeling, and experience together on the page. I live in a New Hampshire landscape of rocks and trees. I experience rocks and trees, I feel rocks and trees, I think about rocks and trees. I did not, however, consciously remember that landscape, and I could not see it from the chair in which I sat. It is such surprises of sight and insight more than anything else that motivate me to write.

When I wrote, "it is a stone tree / a tree stone," I felt I was on the track of something—that I heard a true voice—but I didn't know if I had or what it was saying. There need be no conscious thought at this point in the writing process. These words are not recorded as a result of conscious decision as to their worth, there is no censor at this stage of the process, the pen writes and later the mind considers and reconsiders what the words mean.

During the process of revision the mind is more consciously engaged. We will write nothing but garbage if we do not practice critical thinking towards the end of the writing process, but it is dangerous to be too critical too early. The better educated the writer, the more important it is to suspend the critical element of that education in the early stages of the process. The crimes committed by the writer should, in the beginning, all be unpremeditated. On this early draft I was a dog cocking my ears to a strange and distant sound. Perhaps this sound could be described as a problem to be solved. But I did not rush to attack it. I kept drifting along, my ears cocked, allowing words to appear on my page, seeing the energizing relationships the arrows indicate. Then the timer pinged and I capped the pen, closed the notebook.

After breakfast I went downstairs to my desk, again expecting to work on the novel. But the poem spoke first and I had to turn to the typewriter to see how it would look on the page.

THE LINE
(for John Hatch)

the line comes from what the hand
didn't know it knew

~~the line tells the hand~~
~~what it knew~~

~~this line is a rock~~

this line becomes a rock
that line a tree that cracks a stone

but the tree is not that tree
over there

not ⌠ the rock
     ⌡ ~~the one~~ once seen at Pemaquid

it is a rock on the page
with its own history of frost
ice water earth see tree

this tree
splitting this granite rock
is too real a tree
to be true

the paper flutters to the ground

the hand
makes a rock split by a tree
a rock of halves
no longer remembering each other

the hand tears the paper
from the board
the line leads the hand
across the page

it is not ~~a~~ stone
split by a tree
or a tree splitting
stone

the line shows the hand
a stone tree
a tree stone
not parts but whole ⟵
     that ⟶ face hidden from the eye
          is shown by the ~~line~~ hand
          led by the line

The visual aspect of discovering writing is important but in doing the research for this article I discovered hearing was more important than seeing, at least in creating the draft which marks the dividing line between prewriting and rewriting. I had thought writing appeared on the page, surprising my eye. I intended to describe and probe that process in this article. But in using myself as my own experimental rat, I discovered I heard the writing in my head an instant before it appeared on the page. I was talking to myself when I was writing, listening to what I had to say.

As I realized the importance of this sequence of listening and then seeing, I began to understand why I usually write the first drafts of poems by hand; then, when they seem ready to be tested—to stand by themselves—I type them. It is, I suppose, the first stage in the process of detachment which must take place if a piece of writing is going to move towards its own identity.

The process seems visual, but the words are first heard in my head and the line breaks are first heard, then typed. The lines may change as I read and edit, trying to help the poem arrange itself on the page, but the final test is how the lines sound rather than how they look.

When I started the article I had a subtitle—how language leads to meaning but that doesn't seem to be the process I follow. As my colleague, Professor Thomas Carnicelli, pointed out, my process doesn't seem to be so much linguistic as imagistic, a process of seeing, then recording in language. Rebecca Rule, a writer, added that as the image is written down it is heard more clearly. In this poem I said in those first didactic lines what I intended to explore, then I heard and wrote so I could see what I had heard. As I examine what I usually do as I write, I feel there is a constant productive tension between what is seen and what is said.

Sometimes I fear my literary colleagues, whose business, after all, is critical thinking, want to know what criteria are used in accepting or rejecting a discovered thought as if the criteria were external to the piece of writing. When writers, rather than critics, talk of their own writing to each other and to themselves, they ask what works and what doesn't work. In a real sense they ask the writing what works and listen by reading—often aloud—to the piece of writing's answer. The writer avoids external critical standards—standards which evolved from other pieces of writing in other times by other writers for other readers—and works within the piece of writing. The writer listens to the evolving drafts, "talking with the work" in John Hatch's phrase, to discover its own demands.

Some of what the writer does as he or she reads and rereads, listening to the evolving drafts (and we need careful study of just how writers read drafts), may involve some of the following considerations:

- What information, symbolized by language, is telling us what meaning will evolve? What information clarifies or confirms that evolving meaning?

- What form, order, structure is evolving? What discipline—limits, focus—is the draft imposing on itself?

- What additional information is being attracted to the draft? What more does the writer—and eventually the reader—want to hear from the piece of writing? What questions have to be answered by the piece of writing?

- What does the voice of the draft tell the writer about the writer's point of view towards the subject?

- What is true to the draft? What is the truth—the meaning—of this draft?

It is important, however, that the writer keep such considerations lightly in mind while writing and rewriting, not to think of them too consciously or they will make so much noise the writer will not hear what the piece of writing is telling him or her to write. The writer must let the piece of writing take its own course as much as possible.

As I typed this draft, for example, I was aware I would have a problem deciding between stone and rock, and I was tempted to fiddle with it right away. But I let the draft speak and delayed the decision; I felt the poem would tell me the answer as I turned to the typewriter again.

~~THE LINE~~   THE ROCKTREE
                   (for John Hatch)

~~the line comes from what the hand~~
~~didn't know it knew~~

    this line becomes a rock
    that line a tree that cracks the stone

I continued to type what I heard in my head, extending the poem, but I have not reproduced it all here for the most important changes came in the reading as I listened to the poem, pen in hand. I had typed *rocktree* near the end of the poem. *Rocktree* it was, and the title represented the fact. The exposition at the beginning became unnecessary; it could be cut away. The poem said it was strong enough to begin to speak for itself.

Towards the end of that draft I heard the poem more clearly.

the hand pulls back   not parts but whole
from the line   a nation with a common
                           history of winters

Once   A   ~~the~~ rocktree
remains   hidden from the eye

                           ~~it is not seen by the eye~~
                           ~~but the hand which follows~~
                           ~~the line~~

I saw the artist's hand pull back and that action had to be reported. The pulling back proved to be significant, for the drawing of the rocktree within the poem and the poem itself were detaching themselves from their maker. The flawed and incomplete endings were necessary. They had allowed me to hear the poem in the beginning, but now the scaffolding could begin to be removed. Elizabeth Bowen talks of "what is left after the whittling away of alternatives." Listening to a draft means, in part, paying attention to what belongs, what drives it towards its own meaning.

In the next typing, the poem pulled itself together a bit more, and my ear, listening to the poem, worked out the problem of stone and rock. It was typed again—the fifth draft—and then the Cennini quotation was added in the sixth draft. There were no changes in that final typing, but I could not know that until I typed it and listened to the poem.

> *"this is an occupation known as painting,*
> *which calls for imagination, and skill of hand,*
> *in order to discover things not seen, hiding*
> *themselves under the shadow of natural objects,*
> *and to fix them with the hand, presenting*
> *to plain sight what does not actually exist."*
>
> Cennino Cennini c 1370

THE ROCKTREE
(for John Hatch and Cennino Cennini)

this line becomes a rock
that line a tree that cracks the rock

but the tree is not that tree
over there
not the rock
once seen at Pemaquid

it is a rock
growing out of paper
with its own history of frost
ice water earth seed tree

still
this tree
splitting this granite ledge
is too real a tree
to be true

the paper flutters
to the ground

the hand makes another rock
split by a tree
a rock of halves
no longer remembering each other

the hand tears the paper
from the board

the hand allows the line
to lead the hand

it is not a rock cut by a tree
not a tree that can slice stone

the line shows the hand
not parts but whole
a nation with a common history
of winters

the hand pulls back
from the line

a rocktree
once hidden from the eye
remains
Donald M. Murray

"Rocktree" tells me something I had learned as a writer but did not know until this poem told it to me: the central act of writing is listening.

The experience of the poem also reminded me that I must somehow, as a teacher, a husband, a son, a father, a friend, a colleague, a citizen, a professional, a busy-busy-busy man so proud of my busyness, find time to listen so I will hear what I have to say. If I am able to be quiet within myself something may appear on the page which may become writing and, when that happens, my job is to listen to the evolving writing. The piece of writing will, if I listen carefully, tell me how it needs to be written. It will develop its own shape and form, its own destination, its own voice, its own meaning, and it will finally detach itself from its maker and find readers who may hear things in it I never heard.

It is important we make the student listen to each draft to hear what has to be done—and not done—next. Our normal educational pattern is to tell the students to look to textbooks or to remember lectures although what has been said often bears no relationship to the work at hand and may, in fact, cause the student to tune out what the draft is saying and therefore ruin it. We also counsel students to pay most attention to what they learned from previous writing tasks but each piece of writing has its own history, and each new piece must be listened to as if the writer were writing for the first time.

It may be helpful, however, to articulate some of the questions which published writers no longer need to articulate while they are listening and relistening, writing and rewriting. These questions may help the student to listen to the student's own developing work. Such questions include:

- What did you hear in the draft which surprised you?
- What did you hear that was most interesting?
- What sounds best?
- What sounds so right it can be developed further?
- What is the draft telling you?
- What does the draft ask you to include in it?
- What questions does the draft ask?
- What is the draft trying to say?
- What does the sound of the draft mean?
- In what direction is the order of the information in the draft taking it?
- What is the draft telling you about the subject that you didn't know before?

Too often we tell students to listen to what we have to say when students should listen to their own drafts. These questions can be asked by six-year-old beginning writers and hairy-chinned remedial writers. Neither published writers nor beginning students have much control over what a piece of writing says as it is talking its way towards meaning. Both must listen to the piece of writing to hear where it is going with the same anticipation and excitement we feel when a master storyteller spins out a tale.

In writing this, I realize that listening to a piece of writing is similar to listening to a student in conference, class and workshop. In the beginning, neither the piece of writing nor the student knows what it wants to say. If I listen well and perhaps ask a few questions of the writing I may hear what the writing says in the same way that students in the writing conference or workshop hear what they say when they are given the opportunity to speak of their writing and the process which is producing it. We teach more by listening than by lecturing and we write better if we follow Janwillem van de Wetering's advice to "just write easily, quickly" and listen to what the writing is saying.

This process of listening is more dramatic and easily apparent in poetry than in narrative or in non-fiction, but the process seems more similar in all the forms of writing than it is different—at least the way I write.

When I draft a novel, the making of the draft goes on for months. I stop in the middle of a sentence whenever possible and try to put down three pages of draft a morning, listening to the unfolding story as I hear the words in my head describe the sequence of action and reaction. The process of hearing a novel is the same as hearing a poem.

I also go through a similar process in writing an article such as this. I may do more conscious research and structured thinking in preparation for the writing of non-fiction; I may be aware of a predetermined length or form, a specific audience, an external purpose in writing. Still, I have to listen to the writing as it evolves within those limitations—and if I have a strong piece of writing it may bend those limitations a bit, as it did in the case when I had enough quiet time so that when I thought I was writing a traditional educational article I found I was writing a poem and wrapping an article around it.

Teaching writing is often as unexpected. I must listen and the students must do the talking. That does not mean that I am passive, for the act of listening requires immense concentration and patient receptivity. I must create a climate in the writing conference in which students can hear what they have to say so they can learn to listen to their own writing.

Too often, when we teach writing, we give our students the misconception we plan writing, that we intend what will appear on the page. They are frustrated when they are not able to visualize before the first draft what will appear on their page. The students think they are dumb. We must be honest and let them know how much writing is unconscious or accidental. You do not think writing; you write writing.

Of course, even as I say that, I can think of exceptions. The creative process is never too clear, thank goodness. The elements of intention and planning vary depending on our experience, our purpose, our audience, our writing tasks, but the best writing is often unintended. We usually do not know what we want to say before we say it in non-fiction as well as poetry. We should push ourselves—and our students—to write what they do not expect to say, for the excitement of writing is the surprise of hearing what you did not expect to hear.

I did not expect a rocktree. While dictating the first draft of this article I did not expect to hear my voice developing the relationship between listening to writing and listening to students. But I did hear it, and I recognized its significance. It tied together some things I have learned about writing and about teaching.

I resolve to let my students know why I find it necessary to write quietly for at least fifteen minutes early in the morning. There are 96 quarter-hours in a day, and I need to find at least one quarter hour which I can insulate from busyness so I can listen to myself. If I do that, perhaps I will find a few other quarter hours to listen to the work as it detaches itself from me and tells me what it wishes to become. We write well, not by forcing words on the page, but by listening to those words which collect themselves into a meaning while they are recorded on the page by a good listener.

If our students are to become effective writers, then it is our job to help them find at least a few small slices of quiet time—perhaps in class—and show them how to use that time to listen not to us, but to themselves to hear the writing they did not expect to hear.

six

Voice of the Text

Ever since I was first read to, then started reading to
myself, there has never been a line read that I didn't HEAR.
As my eyes followed the sentence, a voice was saying it
silently to me. It isn't my mother's voice, or the voice of
any person I can identify, certainly not my own. It is
human, but inward, and it is inwardly that I listen to it.
It is to me the voice of the story or the poem itself.

Eudora Welty
One Writer's Beginnings*

We have spent too much time considering the voice of the
writer. That is important but it may be indulgent. What we need to
consider is the voice of the text which combines the writer's voice
with other voices.

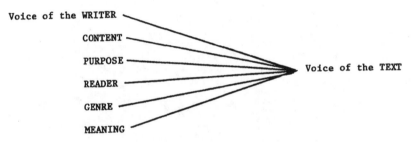

The voice of the writer is the natural voice of a human
being which combines the writer's heritage, environment, genetics,
speaking and writing experience, in a written voice that the reader
can hear. A written voice that can be heard must be written out loud.
The writer must hear the writer's own voice during the writing. The
final text involves the writer's voice adapted to the rhetorical
situation. The writer's voice provides the music which is crucial in
communicating both meaning and feeling to the reader.

The voice of the content limits the voice of the writer. If
we are writing about a rape, the manufacturer of a computer, a hockey
game, there are a range of voices possible in each subject. But that
range is limited. The voice of the content must be appropriate to the
content. The effective writer often adapts his or her voice to the
voices of those who are involved in the subject. The voice captures
the particular music of those who run banks, are on welfare, follow
comets, or sell secondhand cars.

The voice of the purpose is another factor entering into the
voice of the text. We may speak differently when we write to
entertain or persuade, explain or incite.

----
* It is now out in paperback. If you don't have this book, get it.

I have never considered <u>the voice of the reader</u>. I have considered my voice appealing to a reader but the issue seems more complicated to me now. We tune our voices to the voice of the reader, so that readers, reading, will nod, hearing our text in their voices. We enter into their voices, and write for those for whom we write. We give our readers voice.

There is also <u>the voice of the genre</u> or the stylistic tradition of the form of the writing. The range may be enormous, as in the voice of the narrative, smaller in the voice of argument, even smaller in the voice of memoranda. But each genre has its own orchestra of voices. We must write with a voice a reader expects from the genre, and then depart from it if we wish, taking the reader with us. Both the reader and the writer must know the voice of the genre to be surprised and pleased by unexpected variations.

The voice of the text will be changed by the evolving <u>voice of the meaning</u>. What we have to say influences how we will say it. The intellectual and emotional meaning of the text, both affect voice. Meaning is often discovered by voice, and it is communicated by voice.

<u>The voice of the text</u> is the combination of these voices, and much more. As in so many cases in writing, addition becomes multiplication. Six factors do not add up to a simple seventh. The voice of the text is much more than the total of all these factors.

The evolving voice of the text is what tells us how to write. The text itself takes on a mystical quality. When we have a problem in writing – or not writing – we should look to the text. The text will tell us how it needs to be written. The text through writing becomes detached from us and becomes its own entity with its own voice. Listen to Eudora Welty again:

> <u>The writer himself studies intensely how to do it while he is in the thick of doing it; then when the particular novel or story is done, he is likely to forget how; he does well to. Each work is new. Mercifully, the question of HOW abides less in the abstract, and less in the past, than in the specific, in the work at hand...</u>

> <u>Fiction finished has to bear the responsibility of its own meaning, it is its own memory.</u>

> <u>My own words, when I am at work on a story, I hear too as they go, in the same voice that I hear when I read in books. When I write and the sound of it comes back to my ears, then I act to make my changes. I have always trusted this voice.</u>

> <u>At the time of writing, I don't write for my friends or myself either; I write for IT, for the pleasure of IT.</u>

seven

Getting Under the Lightning
(1985)

Writing is primarily not a matter of talent, of dedication, of vision, of vocabulary, of style, but simply a matter of sitting. The writer is the person who writes. The best writing is self-commanded, and most writers have the problems of life: eating, paying the mortgage, getting the kids off to school, responding to those to whom they have commitments. The world intrudes.

Only a handful of writers can attend to their own work full-time. Most writers in the United States hold staff writing jobs, teach, doctor, lawyer, sell, buy, serve society in a way which society will reward with salary—and health benefits.

At times I found it hard to accept this double life, getting up early to write or staying up late when my peers in other professions could lawyer or doctor or insure from eight to five. But then I would remind myself that writing isn't a profession, it is a calling— and the only one calling is yourself. I had no choice; I had to write.

Recently Annie Dillard put all this talk of discipline and work habits in perspective:

> Let me close with a word about process. There's a common notion that self-discipline is a freakish peculiarity of writers—that writers differ from other people by possessing enormous and equal portions of talent and willpower. They grit their powerful teeth and go into their little rooms. I think that's a bad misunderstanding of what impels the writer. What impels the writer is a deep love for and respect for language, for literary forms, for books. It's a privilege to muck about in sentences all morning. It's a challenge to bring off a powerful effect, or to tell the truth about something. You don't do it from willpower; you do it from an abiding passion for the field. I'm sure it's the same in every other field.

Writing a book is like rearing children—willpower has very little to do with it. If you have a little baby crying in the middle of the night, and if you depend only on willpower to get you out of bed to feed the baby, that baby will starve. You do it out of love. Willpower is a weak idea; love is strong. You don't have to scourge yourself with a cat-o'-nine-tails to go to the baby. You go to the baby out of love for that particular baby. That's the same way you go to your desk. There's nothing freakish about it. Caring passionately about something isn't against nature, and it isn't against human nature. It's what we're here to do.

Whether we are motivated by love, hunger for fame, or just plain hunger, the fact is that most of us find it hard to get our rump in the writer's chair and keep it there. I wish more could. I don't need the competition, but most of my students and the teachers with whom I have worked could be writers. But whether they are writers or not, writing is an act of therapy and an act of power. Armed with the craft of writing, each individual can decide to use that craft or not.

Our students have important messages to deliver and their own language in which to deliver them. We need to hear their voices and they need to hear their own voices. I hope the following selections will help make more of those voices heard.

And I hope that by taking the teacher into the writer's studio, the teacher will see the possibility of the powerful interaction I have experienced between practicing my craft and sharing that craft with my students. Each activity has stimulated the other.

D. M.

Writing is easy; it's *not* writing that's hard. The writing comes in a bolt; one moment there is nothing and the next there are a thousand words or more, an always unexpected burst of language that is frightening in the power and complexity of its connections, in the sudden clarity where there was confusion a moment before. It's easy to receive the bolt of lightning when it strikes; what's hard is to create conditions that cause lightning to strike—morning after morning—and then wait for the bolt to hit.

Every six weeks or less I get drawn away from the writing—too many interruptions, too much traveling, too much talking about writing, too many meetings, too much nonwriting writing (letters, memos, handouts)—and I have to reteach myself the conditions that allow me to receive writing. These include:

Sitting

Waiting

Lightning hits twice, thrice, a thousand times in the same spot. Flannery O'Connor teaches and comforts me: "Every morning between 9 and 12 I go to my room and sit before a piece of paper. Many times I just sit for three hours with no ideas coming to me. But I know one thing: If an idea does come between 9 and 12, I am there ready for it." She was a magnificent sitter; I wish I could sit as well as Flannery O'Connor.

But sitting has its price. Watch writers waddle across campus and you'll notice they grow broad in the beam, their spines shaped like a question mark, their necks crane forward as they peer at you. Writers are sedentary hunters. They wait for the lightning and keep making New Year's resolutions to sit better a dozen times a year—each resolution is aimed at getting the rump in *the* chair on a regular basis. My present resolutions:

- *Only* write before lunch.
- *Never* write after lunch.

If I write in the afternoon and the evening—when I don't write very well anyway—I put off all those things that interfere with writing but have to be done. Soon they build up and steal my mornings. Then I don't write and become mean.

Immersion

I am involved with the subjects I write about long before I know I am going to write about them. And I am involved to a degree I cannot demand of my students. I am on duty twenty-four hours a day, reading, observing, absorbing, connecting, thinking, rehearsing. The subjects I write about are never far from me: the death of my daughter, the questions about my family and myself I am still trying to answer, the war in which I learned I could kill, the way I see others and myself behaving toward each other, the process of learning to write.

Of course, I suffer all the guilts that my students admit and my colleagues usually try to hide. I do not read enough; I do not read effectively enough; I do not read what I should read. I'm not up on the latest work—or I do not understand it. And yet I realize that never a day goes by that I am not grabbing hold of new information about the subjects on which I write. I am a continual student, and that is the resource from which all my writing is drawn.

Need

Writing for me is more than a vocation; it is a need; it is the way in which I make meaning of my world, the way I collect and relate, explore and comprehend, speculate and test in a dialogue with myself that never ends. If you don't have to write, don't.

I don't (and didn't) write to win tenure, to get promoted, to make money (with this energy and commitment I could have made eleven killings in real estate). I don't write for fame, since I had a teaspoon of fame early and found it was both irrelevant—the process of doing the writing was long gone and I was doing new work—and unsatisfying—win one award and you want a dozen more.

I write because I have to write. Meet writers and they look ordinary because they are ordinary. It's important for students to become familiar with that ordinariness. We have many writers in our department and our students learn from their ordinariness. "Gee, I look more like a writer than Murray, perhaps I. . . ."

But you'll never know writers as well in person—even lovers, wives, children?—as you'll know them from their writing. And you won't know them from their writing either. The more open and revealing writers are, the more they may be hidden, the more successful at camouflaging their necessary loneliness.

Writers are here and there at the same time, living while observing their living. Talking to you we are also often talking to ourselves in an interior dialogue which discusses—silently, secretly—what is being done while it is being done. Writing, for the writer, is an essential kind of talking to yourself. You may like what you hear, be amused, stirred, stimulated, angered, encouraged, startled, comforted, but what you are hearing is only part of the conversation by which the writer lives. If you don't have to talk to yourself, if you have no need to teach yourself by writing, then writing may not be essential to you. Talk, play the flute, paint, build a bridge, do business, bake, hammer, and do not worry that you're not writing. Society has never said it needed writers. We are all self-appointed and rise to speak without being called upon.

I have no choice. I must write to answer questions I am asking myself, to solve problems that I find interesting, to bring an order into an area where the confusion terrifies me. Donald Barthelme said, "Write about what you're most afraid of," and I nod, smiling. I write to hang on.

Readers

I also write from an external need, to share what I am thinking with that tiny audience of intimates whose respect I need and with whom I am learning. I need to share my writing with my wife, my daughters, Don Graves, Chip Scanlan, Tom Newkirk, Jane Hansen, Carol Berkenkotter (who makes science of pauses, hesitations, and what is left out), and a changing audience of readers, always small, mostly writers themselves, who may respond or not. If hundreds or thousands of other readers tune in later, that's nice, but I really can't see that vague, distant audience who will not see the work until I am two or three projects down the road anyway. Publication is nice, but it is not significant enough to motivate me to place my rear end in the writing chair each morning. I write mostly for myself—and a handful of patient friends.

Critics

I must confess those friendly readers on whom I depend are appreciators mostly. I am too immature to enjoy criticism; more sadist than masochist. I hunger for appreciation, and my writing takes its largest steps forward after praise, not criticism, no matter how much the constructive—or even destructive—comments are deserved. As a teacher I try to remember that.

I find little criticism relevant to the work in progress. Critics usually have their own idea of what I should say—based on their own beliefs—and how I should say it—based on their own ideas of good writing. Even the praise of nonwriting critics has little relationship to the writing in progress, and it can even be destructive— if that's what they think I am saying, I'm really in trouble.

Invitations

When I receive an invitation to write a chapter such as this, to produce a journal article, to give a talk, I try to combine an internal need—how *do* I write—with an external need—maybe students *do* need to know what their teachers practice—and I have a condition for receptivity. The lightning may strike again.

Innocence

I have the advantage in being undereducated for my trade. I'd like to be well educated but I am surrounded by people who are too well educated, who know too well what has been done and what can't be done. If you have the disadvantage of a fine and complete education, move out from that center of comfort to where you don't know everything, where there are dark forests, looming mountains, shadows that move, strange noises in the night.

I write out of what I don't know, not what I know, and that exploration of my ignorance makes each draft, the failed ones even more than the successful ones, fascinating, a challenge for another morning. Of course I keep discovering what others already know—but I have the challenge and the joy of exploration.

Acting

Fragments

I need something to say—an idea, a subject, a theory, a thesis—but what the lightning bolt leaves is usually just a fragment, a puzzling piece of information, a question without an answer, an answer without a question, a detail, an incomplete observation, a partial pattern, an image, a phrase (a fragment of voice), a problem not yet defined, a feeling of anxiety that may be relieved by writing. Writers have learned to pay attention to fragments that others do not even see lying at their feet.

Concentration

Well, yes. Perhaps stubbornness is what I mean, a dumb determination to finish what is started. But that isn't all of it—a good deal of it—but not all of it. With all the necessary distraction and all the unnecessary interruptions, I need to be able, at the time of prewriting and writing, to concentrate on one task over all the others—at least for an hour, an hour and a half, two hours, half an hour, fifteen minutes, ten, less, but still a moment when I fall out of the world, forgetting time, place, duty, and listen to the writing flowing through me to the page.

Deadlines

I have to have deadlines that are self-imposed or imposed by others, and I confess that the deadlines of others are more powerful than my own. I have to be patient, to wait, to listen, not to force the writing, but the day-by-day, hour-by-hour, and louder and louder and louder goose-step march of an approaching deadline is one of the most powerful lightning rods on my study roof.

Planning

I spend most of my time planning what I may write, making lists, making notes, making more lists, talking to myself in my head and in my daybook. I try not to be too formal about how I plan—planning should be, above all, play—and I try not to write too early but wait. I will not force the writing—forced writing sounds like forced writing—but hold back until I have to write. The draft must demand to be written. I want to write when I can*not* not write. When the writing will come easily, without effort.

Drafting

I write fast. I rush forward, writing so fast my handwriting becomes incomprehensible even to me, typing beyond my ability so that the letters and words pile up on the word processor like a train wreck, or dictating so fast I can produce 500 words or 1,000 in an hour; 1,500, 2,000, 2,500, 3,000 in a morning.

The speed itself is important. The best accidents of phrase or meaning—or meaning illuminated by phrase—occur when I am writing too fast.

Rewriting

I'm doing it less and less. Rewriting means the creation of a new draft with major changes in subject, focus, order, voice. These days I plan more and rewrite less. But when I rewrite, I start back at the beginning, seeing the subject anew, not through the vision of the past draft. Rewriting is mostly replanning.

Revising

Of course these first drafts—or third or fourth drafts—will have to be fussed with, cut, added, reordered, shaped, and polished so they appear on the page with the effort hidden, all the spontaneous touches neatly in place. That's fun, once you have a draft in hand.

Voice

Most important of all, voice. I do not begin to write until I hear the voice of the writing, and when that voice fades during the drafting, rewriting/replanning, or revising, I stop, make myself quiet, and listen until I hear it again. The music of the writing, more than anything else, teaches me what I am learning about the subject, what I am feeling about the subject, how I must write the subject to make those thoughts and feelings clear.

And when the writing doesn't go well, the most effective tactic is to listen, quietly, carefully to the writing. If I listen closely enough the writing will tell me what to say and how to say it. As Jayne Anne Phillips says, "It's like being led by a whisper."

Believing

Acceptance

Of what I am, not what I wish I were. Acceptance of the writing I am receiving, remembering that intention is the enemy and surprise the friend. William Stafford (1978) reminds me:

> I can imagine a person beginning to feel that he's not able to write up to that standard he imagines the world has set for him. But to me that's surrealistic. The only standard I can rationally have is the standard I'm meeting right now . . . you should be more willing to forgive yourself. It really doesn't make any difference if you are good or bad today. The *assessment* of the product is something that happens *after* you've done it.

The way I write today is the way I can write today. I must accept what the lightning delivers and make use of it. I can't imagine another text, written by someone other than myself, into being. I must accept myself to write—and accept the fact that writing reveals, not just what I say but who I am. Of course, I am afraid I will be found out—and I will.

Self-consciousness

I used to worry that my compulsive study of my craft—"Don't think" we used to tell the goalie, knowing that if he thought, the puck would be in the net before the decision was made—would paralyze my writing or at least cause terminal constipation. Perhaps it hasn't helped, but I had no choice; long before I taught or made a profession of studying the writing process, I was a student of my craft. Aren't most writers?

Writing is luck but writers are repeatedly lucky. They hit the lottery number again and again. To be a writer, you have to be unself-conscious enough to allow the writing to strike, to allow it to surprise you, to accept the gift. But you have to be prepared—calculatingly prepared—to be lucky, and you have to have the cunning to allow what is written to appear spontaneously in the reader's mind. William Shakespeare: "The truest poetry is the most feigning."

Escaping Craft

Skill is our goal and our prison. We have to learn the tricks of our trade. We apprentice ourselves to our craft to learn to write better—and we do. Our words are surer, stronger; our sentences grow lean; our paragraphs are packed. We learn to turn a phrase, to shape, to polish until our writing becomes professional, polished, slick. Our pieces are so well constructed they say what we have already said—better and better and better until we are hidden within our too well-constructed pages. We are safe. Skilled. Craftpersons. Publishing scholars. Pros.

We have constructed a prison around ourselves with our own carefully crafted words and we can't see out, can't hear out; can't see what needs attending to; can't hear the voice of what we might write on the outside. So we have the obligation to break out, to push beyond our skills, to try and write what we cannot yet write but what needs writing in ways that we have not yet found so that we write with less polish and craft and learn the craft of not finishing the writing too much, to make it rough enough (to leave the roughness in [to remember what Amiri Baraka wrote, "Hunting is not those heads on the wall"]) to let our writing be finished enough so that it helps us do our thinking but not so finished that our readers can only stand and gaze in awe at our clever thinking when we should invite them and allow them to do their own thinking, messing around with our drafts so they will not respect the text too much.

would I stop and mess around with a finished text, unpolish it, unshape it, incomplete it?

you know it
if I can learn how.
know your craft
yeah—that's the complicated thing. Exactly. If I get to know how to do that too well, then I'm crafty again, blinded by my carefully unfinished drafts.

But we *do* want to allow the reader to get into the writing with us, so that the writing doesn't get in the way of the experience of writing/reading reading/writing, so we aren't blinded by the conventions, deafened by the traditions, made dumb by our own hard-earned craft.

unfinishing a text

it is necessary and will be necessary again

as we learn how to get out of the way—how to write rough—when we become crafty enough to allow the writing to appear spontaneous. Even when it is really spontaneous, when we have not got in the way, then what we have done is to learn a new craft, a new skill, a new way of digging in where it is safe and the lightning can never find us. so

Incompleteness

This is a new draft, but it isn't the last word on how writing is made or even how I make writing. It contradicts some things I've said about how I write, and what I say in the future will produce more contradictions. I just wrote a new version of *A Writer Teaches Writing* without opening the previous edition; I am writing a novel without referring to the last draft. I don't want to be imprisoned by my own ideas and my own words. I don't want to be either consistent or proudly inconsistent. I want, each morning to find out what I have to say that day. Each publication is nothing more or less than an entry in my daybook where I talk to myself about what I don't know and need to know, imagining answers to questions that really can't be answered: How do people stay with us after they die? Why did my family do what it did to itself? Why are we able to make war—and to be proud of it? Why did I survive? How do people take experience and re-create it in the minds of others through some squiggles an paper? How do we learn from writing? How can we help others learn to learn from writing? I don't want any questions that have answers—they aren't any fun.

Faith

Hardest of all for me. Faith that I can write, that I have something to say, that I can find out what it is, that I can make it clear to me, to a reader, that I can write so that the reader is not aware of the writer but the meaning.

Faith enough not to read what is written until the entire draft is done and then not to compare it to what might have been or what others have done, but to listen to the writing, to see in it its own meaning, its own form, to hear its own voice. Faith enough to stand out there all alone and invite the lightning.

Witness Trees

When they turned my town from forest
to field, they left one pine standing
at the corners of each clearing,
witness to belonging. These pines
grew old until only they remembered
the great forest, the Indians who moved
under its vast shadow, the cutting,
the burning, the first plowed cut.

The planes take off and I am
lonely witness to the ground that rose
and fell like an ocean from the bombs,
the great flowers of earth and rock
and dirt and blood and bone
that bloomed in war's harvest
when I was young.

4/3/99

eight

Teaching the Other Self
The Writer's First Reader
(1982)

We command our students to write for others, but writers report they write for themselves. "I write for me," says Edward Albee. "The audience of me." Teachers of composition make a serious mistake if they consider such statements a matter of artistic ego alone.

The testimony of writers that they write for themselves opens a window on an important part of the writing process. If we look through that window we increase our understanding of the process and become more effective teachers of writing.

"I am my own first reader," says Issac Bashevis Singer. "Writers write for themselves and not for their readers," declares Rebecca West, "and that art has nothing to do with communication between person and person, only with communication between different parts of a person's mind." "I think the audience an artist imagines," states Vladimir Nabokov, "when he imagines that sort of thing, is a room filled with people wearing his own mask." Edmund Blunden adds, "I don't think I have ever written for anybody except the other in one's self."

The act of writing might be described as a conversation between two workmen muttering to each other at the workbench. The self speaks, the other self listens and responds. The self proposes, the other self considers. The self makes, the other self evaluates. The two selves collaborate: a problem is spotted, discussed, defined; solutions are proposed, rejected, suggested, attempted, tested, discarded, accepted.

This process is described in that fine German novel, *The German Lesson*, by Siegfried Lenz ([1968] 1971), when the narrator in the novel watches the painter Nansen, at work. "And, as always when he was at work he was talking. He didn't talk to himself, he talked to someone by the name of Balthasar, who stood beside him, his Balthasar, who only he could see and hear, with whom he chatted and argued and whom he sometimes jabbed with his elbow, so hard that even we, who couldn't see any Balthasar, would suddenly hear the invisible bystander groan, or, if not groan, at least swear. The longer we stood there behind him, the more we began to believe in the existence of that Balthasar who made himself perceptible by a sharp intake of breath or a hiss of disappointment. And still the painter went on confiding in him, only to regret it a moment later."

Study this activity at the workbench within the skull and you might say that the self writes, the other self reads. But it is not reading as we usually consider it, the decoding of a completed text. It is a sophisticated reading that monitors writing before it is made, as it is made, and after it is made. The term monitor is significant, for reading during writing involves awareness on many levels and includes the opportunity for change. And when that change is made then everything must be read again to see how the change affects the reading.

The writer, as the text evolves, reads fragments of language as well as completed units of language, what isn't on the page as well as what is on the page, what should be left out as well as what should be put in. Even patterns and designs—sketches of possible relationships between pieces of information or fragments of rhetoric or language—that we do not usually consider language are read and discussed by the self and the other self.

It is time researchers in the discipline called English bridge the gulf between the reading researcher and the writing researcher. There are now many trained writing researchers who can collaborate with the trained researcher in reading, for the act of writing is inseparable from the act of reading. You can read without writing, but you can't write without reading. The reading skills required, however, to decode someone else's finished text may be quite different from the reading skills required to chase a wisp of thinking until it grows into a completed thought.

To follow thinking that has not yet become thought, the writer's other self has to be an explorer, a map maker. The other self scans the entire territory, forgetting, for the moment, questions of order or language. The writer/explorer looks for the draft's horizons. Once the writer has scanned the larger vision of the territory, it may be possible to trace a trail that will get the writer from here to there, from meaning identified to meaning clarified. Questions of order are now addressed, but questions of language still delayed. Finally, the writer/explorer studies the map in detail to spot the hazards that lie along the trail, the hidden swamps of syntax, the underbrush of verbiage, the voice found, lost, found again.

Map making and map reading are among man's most complex cognitive tasks. Eventually the other self learns to monitor the always changing relationship between where the writer is and where the writer intended to go. The writer/explorer stops, looks ahead, considers and reconsiders the trail and the ways to get around the obstacles that block that trail.

There is only one way the student can learn map reading—and that is in the field. Books and lecturers may help, but only after the student writer has been out in the bush will the student understand the kind of reading essential for the exploration of thinking. The teacher has to be a guide who doesn't lead so much as stand behind the young explorer, pointing out alternatives only at the moment of panic. Once the writer/explorer has read one map and made the trip from meaning intended to meaning realized, will the young writer begin to trust the other self and have faith it will know how to read other trails through other territories.

The reading writer—map maker and map reader—reads the word, the line, the sentence, the paragraph, the page, the entire text. This constant back-and-forth reading monitors the multiple complex relationships between all the elements in writing. Recursive scanning—or reviewing and previewing—is beginning to be documented during revision by Sondra Perl, Nancy Sommers, and others. But further and more sophisticated investigation will, I believe, show that the experienced writer is able, through the writer's other self, to read what has gone before and what may come afterward during the writing that is done before there is a written text, and during the writing that produces an embryonic text.

I think we can predict some of the functions that are performed by the other self during the writing process.

- The other self tracks the activity that is taking place. Writing, in a sense, does not exist until it is read. The other self records the evolving text.

- The other self gives the self the distance that is essential for craft. This distance, the craftperson's step backwards, is a key element in that writing that is therapeutic for the writer.

- The other self provides an evolving context for the writer. As the writer adds, cuts, or records, the other self keeps track of how each change affects the draft.

- The other self articulates the process of writing, providing the writer with an engineering history of the developing text, a technical resource that records the problems faced and the solutions that were tried and rejected, not yet tried, and the one that is in place.

- The other self is the critic who is continually looking at the writing to see if, in the writer's phrase, "it works."

- The other self also is the supportive colleague to the writer, the chap who commiserates and encourages, listens sympathetically to the writer's complaints and reminds the writer of past success. The deeper we get into the writing process the more we may discover how affective concerns govern the cognitive, for writing is an intellectual activity carried on in an emotional environment, a precisely engineered sailboat trying to hold course in a vast and stormy Atlantic. The captain has to deal with fears as well as compass readings.

We shall have to wait for perceptive and innovative research by teams of reading and writing researchers to document the complex kind of reading that is done during the writing process. But fortunately, we do not have to wait for the results of such research to make use of the other self in the teaching of writing.

The other self can be made articulate. It has read the copy as it was being created and knows the decisions that were made to produce the draft. This does not mean that they were all conscious decisions in the sense that the writer articulated what was being done, but even instinctive or subconscious editorial decisions can be articulated retrospectively.

Many teachers of writing, especially those who are also teachers of literature, are deeply suspicious of the testimony of writers about their own writing. It may be that the critic feels that he or she knows more than the writer, that the testimony of writers is too simple to be of value. But I have found in my own work that what students and professional writers say about their own writing process is helpful and makes sense in relation to the text.

Writing is, after all, a rational act; the writing self was monitored by the reading self during the writing process. The affective may well control or stimulate or limit the cognitive, but writing is thinking, and a thinking act can, most of the time, be recreated in rational terms. The tennis pro may return a serve instinctively, but instinct is, in part, internalized consciousness, and if you ask the pro about that particular return the experienced player will be able to describe what was done and why. If the player thought consciously at the time of the serve, the ball would sail by. The return was a practiced, learned act made spontaneous by experience, and it can be described and explained after the fact.

This retroactive understanding of what was done makes it possible for the teacher not only to teach the other self but recruit the other self to assist in the teaching of writing. The teacher brings the other self into existence, and then works with that other self so that, after the student has graduated, the other self can take over the function of teacher.

When the student speaks and the student and teacher listen they are both informed about the nature of the writing process that produced the draft. This is the point at which the teacher knows what needs to be taught or reinforced one step at a time, and the point at which the student knows what needs to be done in the next draft.

Listening is not a normal composition teacher's skill. We tell and they listen. But to make effective use of the other self the teacher and the student must listen together.

This is done most efficiently in conference. But before the conference at the beginning of the course the teacher must explain to the class exactly why the student is to speak first. I tell my students that I'm going to do as little as possible to interfere with their learning. It is their job to read the text, to evaluate it, to decide how it can be improved so that they will be able to write when I am not there. I point out that the ways in which they write are different, their problems and solutions are different, and that I am a resource to help them find their own way. I will always attempt to underteach so that they can overlearn.

I may read the paper before the conference or during the conference, but the student will always speak first in the conference. I have developed a repertoire of questions—what surprised you? what's working best? what are you going to do next?—but I rarely use them. The writing conference is not a special occasion. The student comes to get my response to the work, and I give my response to the student's response. I am teaching the other self.

The more inexperienced the student and the less comprehensible the text, the more helpful the writer's comments. Again and again with remedial students I am handed a text that I simply can not understand. I do not know what it is supposed to say. I can not discover a pattern of organization. I can not understand the language. But when the writer tells me what the writer was doing, when the other self is allowed to speak, I find that the text was produced rationally. The writer followed misunderstood instruction, inappropriate principles, or logical processes that did not work.

Most students, for example, feel that if you want to write for a large audience you should write in general terms, in large abstractions. They must be told that is logical; but it simply doesn't work. The larger the audience, the more universal we want our message to be, the more specific we must become. It was E. B. White who reminded us, "Don't write about Man, write about *a* man."

When the teacher listens to the student, the conference can be short. The student speaks about the process that produced the draft or about the draft itself. The teacher listens, knowing that the effective teacher must teach where the student is, not where the teacher wishes the student was, then scans or rescans the draft to confirm, adjust, or disagree with the student's comments.

One thing the responsive teacher, the teacher who listens to the student first then to the text, soon learns is that the affective usually controls the cognitive, and affective responses have to be dealt with first. I grew used to this with students, but during the past two years I have also worked with professionals on some of the best newspapers in the country, and I have found that it is even more true of published writers. Writers' feelings control the environment in which the mind functions. Unless the teacher knows this environment the teaching will be off target.

In conference, for example, the majority of men have been socialized to express a false confidence in their writing. The teacher who feels these men are truly confident will badly misread the writer's other self. The behavior of women in conference is changing, but not fast enough. Most women still express the false modesty about their accomplishments that society has said is appropriate for women. Again the teacher must recognize and support the other self that knows how good the work really is.

I am constantly astonished when I see drafts of equal accomplishment, but with writer evaluations that are miles apart. One student may say, "This is terrible. I can't write. I think I'd better drop the course." And right after that on a similar paper a student says, "I never had so much fun writing before. I think this is really a good paper. Do you think I should become a writer?"

Many students, of course, have to deal first with these feelings about the draft—or about writing itself. The conference teacher should listen to these comments, for they often provide important clues to why the student is writing—or avoiding writing—in a particular way.

The instructor who wishes to teach the other self must discuss the text with that other self in less despairing or elated tones. Too often the inexperienced conference teacher goes to the polar extreme and offers the despairing student absolute praise and the confident student harsh criticism. In practice, the effective conference teacher does not deal in praise or criticism. All texts can be improved, and the instructor discusses with the student what is working and can be made to work better, and what isn't working and how it might be made to work.

As the student gets by the student's feelings, the concerns become more cognitive. At first the students, and the ineffective writing teacher, focus on the superficial, the most obvious problems of language or manuscript preparation. But the teacher, through questioning, can reorient the student to the natural hierarchy of editorial concerns.

These questions over a series of conferences may evolve from "What's the single most important thing you have to say?" to "What questions is the reader going to ask you and when are they going to be asked?" to "Where do you hear the voice come through strongest?"

The students will discover, as the teacher models an ideal other self, that the largest questions of content, meaning, or focus have to be dealt with first. Until there is a clear meaning the writer can not order the information that supports that meaning or leads towards it. And until the meaning and its supporting structure is clear the writer can not make the decisions about voice and language that clarify and communicate that meaning. The other self has to monitor many activities and make sure that the writing self reads what is being monitored in an effective sequence.

Sometimes teachers who are introduced to teaching the other self feel that listening to this student first means they can not intervene. That is not true. This is not a do-your-own-thing kind of teaching. It is a demanding teaching, it is nothing less than the teaching of critical thinking.

Listening is, after all, an aggressive act. When the teacher insists that the student knows the subject and the writing process that produced the draft better than the teacher, and then has faith that the student has an other self that has monitored the producing of the draft, then the teacher puts enormous pressure on the student.

Intelligent comments are expected, and when they are expected they are often received.

I have been impressed by how effectively primary students, those in the first three grades in school, have a speaking other self. Fortunately this other self that monitors the writing process has been documented on tape in a longitudinal study conducted in the Atkinson, New Hampshire, schools by Donald Graves, Lucy Calkins and Susan Sowers at the University of New Hampshire. There the other self has been recorded and analyzed.

The most effective learning takes place when the other self articulates the writing that went well. Too much instruction is failure centered. It focuses on error and unintentionally reinforces error.

The successful writer does not so much correct error as discover what is working and extend that element in the writing. The writer looks for the voice, the order, the relationship of information that is working well, and concentrates on making the entire piece of writing have the effectiveness of the successful fragment. The responsive teacher is always attempting to get the student to bypass the global evaluations of failure—"I can't write about this," "It's an airball," "I don't have anything to say," and move into an element that is working well. In the beginning of a piece of writing by a beginning student that first concern might well be the subject or the feeling that the student has toward the subject. The teacher may well say, "Okay. This draft isn't working, but what do you know about the subject that a reader needs to know?"

Again and again the teacher listens to what the student is saying—and not saying—to help the student hear that other self that has been monitoring what isn't yet on the page or what may be beginning to appear on the page.

This dialogue between the student's other self and the teacher occurs best in conference. But the conferences should be short and frequent.

"I dunno," the student says. "In reading this over I think maybe I'm more specific." The teacher scans the text and responds, "I agree. What are you going to work on next?" "I guess the ending. It sorta goes on." "Okay. Let me see it when it doesn't."

The important thing is that only one or two issues are dealt with in a conference. The conference isn't a psychiatric session. Think of the writer as an apprentice at the workbench with a master workman, a senior colleague, stopping by once in a while for a quick chat about the work.

We can also help the other self to become articulate by having the student write, after completing a draft, a brief statement about the draft. That statement can be attached on the front of the draft so the teacher can hear what the other self says and respond, after reading that statement and the draft, in writing. I have found this far less effective than the face-to-face conference, where the act of listening is personal, and where the teacher can hear the inflection and the pause as well as the statement and where the teacher can listen with the eye, reading the student's body language as well as the student's text.

The other self develops confidence through the experience of being heard in small and large group workshops. The same dynamics take place as have been modeled in the conference. The group leader asks the writer, "How can we help you?" The other self speaks of the process or of the text. The workshop members listen and read the text with the words of the other self in their ears. Then they respond, helping the other self become a more effective reader of the evolving text.

The papers that are published in workshops should be the best papers. The workshop members need to know how good writing is made, and then need to know how good writing can be improved. I always make clear that the papers being published in workshops are the best ones. As the other self speaks of how these good papers have been made and how they can be improved, the student being published has the student's most effective writing process reinforced. You can hear the other self becoming stronger and more confident as it speaks of what worked and as it proposes what may work next. The other workshop members hear an effective other self. They hear how a good writer reads an evolving draft. And during the workshop sessions their other selves start to speak, and they hear their own other selves participate in the helpful process of the workshop.

The teacher must always remember that the student, in the beginning of the course, does not know the other self exists. Its existence is an act of faith for the teacher. Sometimes that is a stupendous act of faith. Ronald, his nose running, his prose stalled, does not appear to have a self, and certainly not a critical, constructive other self. But even Ronald will hear that intelligent other self if the teacher listens well.

The teacher asks questions for which the student does not think there are answers: Why did you use such a strong word here? How did you cut this description and make it clearer? Why did you add so many specifics on Page 39? I think this ending really works, but what did you see that made you realize that old beginning was the new ending?

The student has the answers. And the student is surprised by the fact of answers as much as the answers themselves. The teacher addresses a self that the student didn't know exists, and the student listens with astonishment to what the other self is saying— "Hey, he's not so dumb." "That's pretty good, she knows what she's doing."

The teacher helps the student find the other self, get to know the other self, learn to work with the other self, and then the teacher walks away to deal with another Ronald in another course who does not know there is another self. The teacher's faith is building experience. If Ronald had another self, then there is hope for faith.

What happens in the writing conference and the workshop in which the other self is allowed to become articulate is best expressed in the play, *The Elephant Man,* by Bernard Pomerance, when Merrick, the freak, who has been listened to for the first time in his life, says, "Before I spoke with people, I did not think of all those things because there was no-one to think them for. Now things come out of my mouth which are true."

nine

Like Orwell, Essaying One's Best
(1995)

Don's weekly Boston Globe *column dealt mainly with issues of aging. In covering that beat, that subject area, Don sometimes discussed writing and other forms of making art, seeing these as ways everyone could find the surprise and comfort that he found in reading, writing, sketching, and painting.*

The other morning, when my words lay sodden on the page, I once more apprenticed myself to George Orwell. I searched through the pages of my *Collected Essays, Journalism and Letters of George Orwell*, by Sonia Orwell and Ian Angus (1968), seeking instruction and inspiration from such essays as:

"England Your England"
As I write, highly civilized human beings are flying overhead, trying to kill me.

"Marrakech"
As the corpse went past the flies left the restaurant table in a cloud and rushed after it, but they came back a few minutes later.

"Reflections on Gandhi"
Saints should always be judged guilty until they are proved innocent.

"Shooting an Elephant"
In Moulmein, in Lower Burma, I was hated by large numbers of people—the only time in my life that I have been important enough for this to happen to me.

98

I was instructed and inspired, but not in the way I expected. In tracking down the famous openings of these essays in the 2,014 pages of the collection, I read dozens of beginnings that were as limp or as clumsy as mine. I'm no George Orwell, but neither was George Orwell most days.

We need to remember that our friend's house, neat for company, was ripe with old newspapers, dog hair and a pizza coffin from the night before. Most of us measure our worst against another's best.

A friend of mine once played golf with Ben Hogan in his prime and was surprised that their score was close. It was after the game that he noticed the difference between them. Hogan took 400 golf balls and hit 100 on each of four key shots he had missed.

George Orwell not only wrote great essays because of talent honed by craft, but because he wrote. He filled the page, day after day, year after year, practicing his craft so that he was prepared for inspiration when it dropped by.

He also submitted and published the worst while waiting for the best.

Many of us in retirement have the time to pursue our dreams, but we have to relearn the lessons of the crafts that are paying for our retirement.

We have to remember the miles of visits that produced no sales as well as the few visits that paid off; we have to remember the loaves of bread that did not rise before the one that did.

These days I am the poet I wanted to be at 18. Now I write the poems I imagined for most of the decades between college and retirement, but not many get in the mail. And if they are not in the mail, they are not rejected—or published.

In retirement I wanted to become the artist I never was. I have shelf after shelf of books on art; drawers filled with pens, pencils, brushes, paints, crayons, charcoal, watercolors, oils; stacks of sketchbooks, paper, canvas.

What I do not have is stacks of drawings and paintings. I haven't found—made—the time.

And as a writer I know that talent depends on abundance, the accumulation of work that is good and bad.

In fact, Orwell may not have liked the essays I most admire and may have been most proud of some of those I pass as ordinary.

The artist often does not know what the world will like. The symphony the composer sees as a failure because it did not achieve his ambition for it may be the one that is played long after he is gone.

The painting, the play, the book, the newspaper column the maker likes the best may be ignored, while the work that is struck off in haste—after a lifetime of apprenticeship to the maker's craft—may be the one that is remembered.

That used to disturb me, but now it offers comfort. The true satisfaction is in the making of the work.

At the moment of making, the writer, painter, composer, golfer, baker or quiltmaker enjoys the gift of concentration. And as we age, that gift increases in importance.

We are fortunate when we are lost to the world and are too old to suffer the ambition of fame. We are blessed, as Orwell was, when we focus on the small, immediate demands of the work at hand.

This stitch, this dough, this cast, this drive, this melody, this line, this word becomes our momentary universe.

Orwell wasn't, with such a moment, the famous writer, but simply a writer trying to find the right word and fit it into a line that made meaning clear.

And I do not have to be George Orwell any more than he has to be George Orwell. All I have to do is to concentrate on this line, then the next.

ten

Writing Badly to Write Well

Searching for the Instructive Line
(1984)

As I indicate in the following article, I thought Don Daiker was joking when he invited me to speak before a conference of sentence combiners. I was challenged, however, by the unexpected opportunity and accepted; then, as the date grew closer, I was terrified—a common sequence. I decided to have fun by establishing a technical problem to solve. My friend, novelist Thomas Williams, once pointed out to me that the writer is often stimulated by solving a technical problem—for example, writing in the present tense or never using a flashback in fiction. The reader shouldn't be aware of these technical challenges most of the time, but it helps drive the writer forward.

I decided to combine sentences, pile up huge train wrecks of clauses, and have fun with the language as well as the content of the piece. I read it to the audience, which I rarely do, because of the complexity of the writing. And they got it. They understood it and laughed with me, not at me.

D. M.

Not yet in the notebook; in the head:

I want to celebrate first—then analyze, understand, explain?— the instructive line that leads me to the meanings I make—to the meanings I have the need to make—but to celebrate I have to write what I celebrate (well enough to make it a celebration), not to look back afterwards to what someone else has done—some great dead writer who has burned his drafts—but to write writing, following lines searching for a meaning before they really are even lines, to begin to understand how those lines work, as they drag me toward

their own meaning, product of my experience and my past thinking but freed—if the line works—from that into becoming what I
have not yet thought.

It rarely works clearly—or obviously—but it works. This
cleaned up thinking, thinking after I know I am thinking, late prethinking but still a kind of thinking—a kind of thinking important
for our students to know about—that we think as confusedly as
they do, when we are lucky, if our education still allows it (remember that Snodgrass poem "The Examination"), they should see it
in action, not because they have to learn it, they *know* it, but
because they should be allowed it, because by playing with the
line, no, by listening for, no, to the line (((that I know will come if
I am quiet and prepared to listen ((it is damn hard to listen for
what you do not expect to hear—do not want to hear, even fear of
hearing (my mother-in-law always responded to what she expected
me to say rather than what I said: "The house is on fire." "Isn't
that nice.") but a lot more fun: if I knew what I was going to write,
I wouldn't write)) because I have learned to listen before, in other
writing, and in listening heard))) it will come and drag me from
word through phrase and fragment and line to a meaning that may
be tested and made clear by being turned into a sentence.

That is neither beginning nor ending. It is writing writing, writing
in the act of writing, not writing written but lines searching for a
meaning, a beagle running this way and that through my mind,
nose to the ground, tail high, busy, busy, busy.

I thought the invitation a joke. Somebody was impersonating
Don Daiker inviting me to a meeting of sentence combiners, a
rabbi invited to a Nazi rally. But I called back. It was Don Daiker
and he was serious. We want you because you are not a true
believer. Such an invitation; such chutzpah to accept. Of course I
would address the rally.

And would I suggest a title? Well, the sentence might be appropriate, the sentence seen from the inside, trying to tug the writer
along on the search for meaning: "Following Language Toward
Meaning." Language, not sentence, some instinct gave me room.

Glad I did. I want to deal with something less and more than a sentence: the line.

Poets talk about the line, not the sentence or the verse. Modern poets, anyway. Valery's line given. Of course the line has a validity in poetry, modern poetry anyway. Line breaks, that sort of stuff. The line is the basic unit, comes as a fragment. My poems are prose I suppose first but as Charlie Simic says, "Last fall I did a lot of poems. Not really poems, but something that looked like poems." I write stuff that looks like poetry. But isn't. It has lines, but they don't break the right way, they are prosey (prosy?), too much like sentences. The poems are in the fragments. Pieces of pottery lying around from which a poem may be built. Chunks of language (Frank O'Hare jammed up against me as we rode in the backseat of a car in San Francisco, talking about chunks. Didn't find out what he meant really. Glad I didn't, freed me up to think about chunks my own way), space debris drifting by, thoughts, no, almost thoughts, not yet thoughts, images, chunks, stuff when meditating, something to catch your eye or ear but never looked at head on, a state of half seeing, half listening, recording. If you pay too much attention, you'll miss it. To find the right language, at least the beginning of the right language, you have to train yourself to inattention ("Donald, stop staring out the window."), not to listen too well.

Many teachers complain that their students can't write sentences. I complain that many of my students write sentences. Too early. Following form, forgetting meaning. Following language toward correctness. For its own sake. Sentences that are like prison sentences. They don't unlease meaning, they contain meaning, compress meaning, squeeze the meaning out of language and leave me with the juiceless skins and pulp, enough of that, but then I too have those who don't write sentences when they should, well, to hell with that now. Now I am in praise of bad sentences, stuff that isn't ready to be sentences and wouldn't be helped by becoming sentences. Now. At this time. Premature births. But births. Living.

We don't know enough about how to write badly—and why. Syntax often breaks down when we approach a new and interesting meaning, something we have thought before or are afraid of thinking or sabotages what we had thought before and, God forbid, said at an academic meeting or, worse still, had published. I am surprised when they take me seriously when I guess and write what I don't yet know. But I don't have to take myself as seriously. I must make sure I'm not glib and professional—at least at the wrong times. Polished, the meaning all rounded and shaped and shining until it is no meaning at all.

Ed Corbett told my wife he was astonished that I spoke extemporaneously and that all my sentences parsed. My reactions were immediate. I would never speak again. Someone was keeping score. It isn't true, it can't be true. Maybe it is. I mean, Ed Corbett, if anyone knows such a thing, Ed Corbett does. Wow. Great. Terrible. That's what worries me most about speaking. It comes out so neatly, and the audience likes that, naturally, and you get warm and wiggle all over when they respond but it's too neat, parsed, all contained.

Well, isn't writing? Yes, but, I hope, I think, there is a difference. Speaking involves a lot of tricks you can't get away with in writing. Writing can be examined, read back, studied. But it is a worry that the meaning will be made too clear, that sentences will eliminate doubt and questioning and contradictions. Perhaps we will succeed, think of that, and our students will think clearly all the time. What's the definition of a demigod, a dictator, a nonthinker? One who thinks clearly all the time. We need to teach unclear thinking. Perry—and others—Elbow looping away madly, Macrorie, others, are aware that the young often think too clearly, see everything in black and white, precisely, every effect having its cause. What if we give them the language patterns into which they can fit these prematurely clear thoughts.

Well, certainly my students . . . I know. Perhaps we need a grammar of bad writing or unfinished writing, a codification of those ways . . . Whoops. Well, at least we need to find out how we write the nonsentences that made meaning-full sentences possible. Now, you're talking. Is this like jazz improvisation? Sort of. Probably yes. There's experience and tradition but the need to push the edges, to go beyond, to fail. I've got to fail more in my writing. You say: "You've made it in this piece." Good.

I accept the assignment. And my mind knows it is going to have to work on that. I don't think. My head does better if it is left alone. It will make its own connections, become aware when something is said or read that may fit. But some stuff surfaces in the daybooks. Often it is diagrams but not in this case. It isn't often free writing written down. Free writing isn't free enough, at least for me. It takes over or perhaps my professionalism takes over and it begins to shape, encompass, enclose, tighten up, screw down, compress, refine, limit. A lot of what follows are fragments, drafts for titles, one-line drafts of the talk that may become a chapter. Such title fragments are typical of my planning for writing. They seem to lead me. Perhaps they are abstractions for free writing or free thinking. Signposts pointing toward meaning. Tracks. Clues. Perhaps more. Lines. A kind of shorthand which allows me to see where I may go. Not sentences. Not even uncombined sentences. Not yet.

What do I see in them, hear in them? Voice and dance. I listen to what they say and how they say it, watch to see how they move.

Connections. Attractions and resistances. Tension. Especially tension, forces that are working against each other but not escaping each other. Marriages of ideas. Ideas I've had but haven't forced together yet. Ideas that can't escape each other but are uncomfortable with each other in an interesting way. Forces that react with each other to create something that is more—or different—than they are alone. At least when it works. It works when it is on the edge of not working but still does, sort of, at least.

How can we define the line?

The line is a word or a series of words that points the writer toward a potential meaning.

Note that the line has one reader: the writer. The line need only communicate to the writer, and therefore the line is often made up of code words that have private meanings that appear general, vague, or cliché to other readers but which are loaded with precise meanings for the writer.

Calvin Trillin says, "I do a kind of pre-draft—what I call a 'vomit-out.' . . . It degenerates fairly quickly, and by page four or five sometimes the sentences aren't complete. . . . I have an absolute terror of anybody seeing it. It's a very embarrassing document. I tear it up at the end of the week." Fair enough for Trillin. He's not a teacher. He's a stylist, writes for the *New Yorker*, makes me sick he writes so good, so easily, so trippingly on the tongue. But if he were my teacher I'd need to see those "vomit-out" drafts; I'd need to learn to write as badly as he does and then learn to work from there to the pieces that are published, the examples of what looks like effortless craft.

These are random selections. They were written in bunches or alone, spread out in:

THE DAYBOOKS 24–32, OCTOBER 6, 1982–OCTOBER 11, 1983:
uncombining sentences
how sentences lead to meaning
following language to meaning
language leads to meaning
chunks, sentences and paragraphs
learning to follow language
breakdown of syntax
how combining and uncombining lead to new meaning
teaching on the student's text
need for rebellious sentences
let your sentences rebel
sentences that make their own meaning
how sentences find their meaning
let sentences lead you to meaning
incorrect sentences may lead to meaning
sentences that don't work may think
sentences reflect thought already thunk
people don't think in sentences

need sentences that betray thought, cause vision, surprise,
    anger, twist and turn toward their own meaning not mine
find ways to study language in search of meaning so students
    will be able to write uncorrect sentences which
William Carlos Williams:
        "I am that he whose mind is scattered
        aimlessly."
celebrate the prose line—the sentence
line—the sentence—leads to meaning
grows its own laws out of its own need to make meaning
must consider the line before the sentence—the fragment
ends of lines
how a sentence makes meaning
the magic of the line
the prose line
a celebration of the prose line
energizing line
inspiring line
insightful line
fragment to sentence
the teaching line
the instructive line
the instructing line
the suggestive line
finding the instructive line
seeking the instructive line
hunting for the instructive line
hearing the instructive line
      listening
      lying in wait
        3 stages
          given line
          following, leading line
          in (something) sentence
celebrate the prose line
      less and more than a sentence
a celebration of the prose line

adventures with the prose line
following the prose line toward meaning
from word to phrase to sentence to meaning
from word to phrase to line to meaning
from word to line to meaning
how line leads to meaning
how the prose line leads to meaning
how the prose line may lead to meaning.

A year of fragments. How does the prose line teach (instruct) me? It is a way of thinking, not thought then writing, not even thinking in language within my head ((often I think in pictures (images) and in patterns (designs)) but thinking by seeing what I have written.

But since here my research and my thinking are *about* the line, I must use the line.

Let's share a line trying to find its meaning. This was not written before. It is being written now. The line that beckons me—the dead will not stay put in their graves—has passed by before, a fragment of feeling from my autobiography, a fragment that has anger in it and guilt at the anger. I don't particularly want to deal with it, but it is attaching itself to me. And it may be poetry. I don't want to write poetry here and now, but again I seem to have no choice.

the dead will not stay put in their graves
the dead will not in the grave
the dead will not stay
underground
out of sight
where they who have deserted me
belong

the dead will not stay put
in their graves
underground and out of sight
I expected memories and of course

108

a certain sadness
but not this
ghosts would be better than
this
not knowing
if the dead are dead or I am alive

My father, trailing wires, that box still strapped to his chest
still smiles. Without his glasses, I cannot still read his eyes,
get behind the smile. Tear the mask. Am I him now,
bearded, smiling, just as masked to my children—my wife,
my students, friends? He would tell anyone, it seemed, too
much of himself, selling himself instead of his damned
ladies hosiery. And now I am open, too, but what can
anyone see in this openness. Am I what they see or do they
see what they need to see.

I play all the parts
to (my) children the father
to the wife a husband
to parents son
to students teacher
neighbors neighbor

I play every part
to my children the father
to my wife the husband
to parents son
students teacher
neighbors neighbor
and to my friends the
      mirror
they need to see
      themselves
as they need to be seen
until at night I take off
the masks the costumes
speak no lines

This trails off. Perhaps it will draw me back. Perhaps not. No
matter. It looked liked poetry, became prose, then poetry again, but
it was really no genre yet. It was pre-genre, pre-form, and all the
courses we teach that demand form before meaning (always virtu-
ous, always justifiable, always neater than the writing experience).

Yes, often correct, appropriate. I *teach* nonfiction (although I write fiction and poetry and nonfiction), but we run the danger of closing down thinking, exploration, and discovery if we pay too much attention to genre at the wrong time. The line will lead us to the form. And should. And our students must have the experience of writing what they do not expect to write. That is the essential writing experience, and if you do not feel that firsthand, you cannot understand writing.

The line is more open than the sentence. It is still searching for the meaning that it does not yet have. It may be important for the student writer to discover there is a legitimate pre-sentence with which to work, play, sketch possible meanings.

Writing fast is a component of free writing but it must be separated from free writing. Writing fast is one important way to draft because it frees the writer from notes, research, outline, prethinking and encourages language to race ahead of the writer seeking a precise meaning. This is not free writing for there is a goal, the subject of the piece being written. All the planning, rehearsal, research is there—in fact, all those activities prime the writer and make meaning-searching language possible. I have gone to sleep knowing not what I will say but what I will say about—the topic or the point of view or the feeling felt or sort of half thoughts not dragged from the subconscious but disturbed a bit to make them, to stimulate them, like the farmer who loosened his tomato plants "to scare them" and make them hurry up their producing, and then I wake up knowing I will be writing and what I will be writing about but still not allowing sentences, just protecting the feeling of the writing from language, only half listening to TV and half reading the newspaper and really not writing so I can go downstairs and allow the language to come in such a way it will surprise me and tell me, because of its speed, I'm like Faulkner said, a writer is "like a man building a chicken coop in a high wind. He grabs onto any board he can and nails it down fast" so I will be able to step back from my chicken coop and see what I have built. This speed is most apparent when I am dictating and we have all had the same experience speaking in class, rare, but enough, and we hear ourselves saying what we did not expect to say, better than we expected to say, and that is one reason I dictate to get the speed to force my writing beyond my thinking although I'm not dictating this but it comes out in sentences too often and so I'll push myself like this with the word processor, trying to get ahead of syntax so I will write what I do not expect to write and all my education and experience and publishing, all my professional glibness, gets out of the way and I do not do it often enough.

You *do* have to write badly to write well. Of course. Badly in the sense of neatness and completeness, for effective thinking isn't neat and complete. This word processor thinks neat and complete. It is dumb, everything is programmed. It follows orders, everything is a simple matter of yes or no. We think by leaps, by inference and intuition, by hunch, guess and accident, especially accident. When I studied and did not learn watercoloring, the teacher said we had to rationalize our accidents. We needed material that would cause accidents and we had to have the experience to increase our accidents. Yes, writing is like that. We have to be able to have productive accidents and to be able to perceive in the mess what is worthy of rationalization, what has to be thought about. Writers are a very special kind of reader; they have to be able to do a special kind of reading, reading what isn't there yet, what may be developed and then shaped and polished with sentences into something that others can read not like this but a nice meaning that may, unfortunately, seem more than this jumble but be, in fact, less because of all the polishing. Yes, I like Linda Flower's writer-based and reader-based prose but I guess what we have, what I teach, what I force is often too much reader-based prose when the writing I most admire that stretches me because it stretched the writer is writer-based prose, writing that continues to search for a meaning after it leaves the writer's desk and can we tolerate it then in our composition classes? Well I don't at least not for a grade at the end and I guess I shouldn't but then perhaps I'm cheating my students if I don't do something to let them loose. We all have students who write too well, don't we, who are uptight, imprisoned in themselves or write with too much ease, parsing their way toward suitable meanings, what was it Joubert said, "To write well, one needs a natural facility and an acquired difficulty." Yes, that sort of thing, language fitting together with an instructive roughness, no polish yet.

I am drawn back to that haunting line—the dead will not stay put in their graves—which has, within it, an interesting tension that may describe a feeling that many of us have at times. There is, in the line, strong feeling, perhaps anger, and there is a surprise in the action and reaction between the words. We usually think that the dead stay in their graves but here's a line telling us they do not and, more than that, the line has an opinion about it. Not an Easter-like celebration—they are risen—or pleasure, or fear, but a kind of impatience that they are not behaving properly. It will be interesting to see where that line may take me this time.

THE DEAD WILL NOT STAY DEAD
Grandma sits up
    half lying the way she was propped
    against her pillows
    she's been watching
    disapproving

Mother is curled away from me
    or is it father
    from whom she turns
    this enormous woman
    always child to her mother
    sucks her thumb

Father still smiles
    he's still the deacon
    usher at funerals
    floorwalker salesman
    hidden behind the well-pressed suit
    starched collar moustache
    smile

Lee waves
> she seems as surprised
> as we were that she went first
> but does not seem unhappy waiting
> she was always the sunny one
> and she still tries to comfort us

Look. I did not want to write about that, to confront the ghosts, to feel the loss, to share it, to expose it to myself, to others, the bad writing, the uncomfortable feelings, is it self-pity, and am I exploiting my family, embarrassing readers? I don't want to expose myself to myself and, in fact, I expected to write a line that would begin a story or an essay on this subject, to stand at a distance from it, but I must write where language takes me. I must be open to the night dreams and daydreams, the thoughts that wander behind my own protective, salesman's smile, hiding what I am thinking from others but not myself.

There are things in the lines that surprise and intrigue me. Mother turning away, for example, curled up as a baby as I once saw her during her dying, when I became parent to my parents and they children to me. But then another line comes to me out of nowhere. No, not a line, a picture of the baby of close friends. My wife and I had dropped by their home the day before and visited for a few minutes, delighting in their joy at their little girl.

> Caitlin is seven months old
> and she stands wobbley legged
> looks back over her shoulder
> black-eyed woman already
>
> we talk of how fast she learns
> to stand explore judge
> charm to be herself in a world
> that tries to make her fit
>
> (I am stunned at what Caitlin knows)

(what Caitlin knows
she has come so recently from death
born into living)

(what Caitlin knows
so recently arrived
from Death)

(what Caitlin knows
of Death from where she came
she will not tell
but celebrates her living)

(touching tasting
reaching out)

WHAT CAITLIN KNOWS
at seven months
and standing wobble
  legged
looking back over her
  shoulder
woman already
	WHAT CAITLIN KNOWS
	at seven months
	standing wobble legged
	
	looking back over her
	  shoulder
	woman already

how fast she learns we say watching her crawl touch taste search reject	how fast she learns we say as she crawls beyond the rug to recapture
and charm	the yellow plastic ring

forgetting how much
  knowing
she brings from Death
which can't be darkness
if she smiles
  remembering
	forgetting the knowing
	
	she brings from Death
	  (we should remember
	what she does smiling)

I must stop and not follow language where it takes me. Not this morning. I have a paper to write. I look at the clock. For the first time in twenty years of teaching I have written right through a student conference. The line has concentrated all my attention on that moment and its meaning. I have gone from death to birth and perhaps beyond. It felt good and it was exciting—following the line. But I don't know whether I have written well or not. Don't care. That is unimportant. But I have followed a line toward an unexpected meaning and it's happened right here (it's all here) and I hope the reader—the listener—can feel just a bit of the excitement I felt when I intended to write prose and found that the line was leading me to poetry, or something that might become poetry, and that when I wrote of death I found myself moving from those ghosts that haunt me to Caitlin Fisher and to the experience yesterday afternoon when I sat on the floor and enjoyed her and enjoyed her parents' and my wife's and my own enjoyment of her. And my language pulled me toward an understanding that surprises me. It may not be a great thought for someone else, but it wasn't so much a thought for me as a perception, an understanding, an experience, a realization that she came—so full of life, so happy—from where my Lee is and where we all go, and somehow the feeling that it can't be so bad if Caitlin arrived so full of happiness.

What is the instructive line? What is it in a line that leads me on, that teaches me that meaning may lie ahead? Well, it's not something that I think about normally; it's something I do. If you think about hitting a curve, you won't. And so I don't think about it. But if the batter becomes a coach? Alright, I have to think about it. To make money I am led to arrogance. I presume to teach, to find out what I do, and then, no matter how embarrassing, or unacademic and unprofound and unintellectual, to expose it, to reveal what is simple and obvious to others. And then to be surprised, for it isn't, apparently, quite so obvious—and perhaps not so simple.

- I listen to the line. In fact, I hear it rather than see it. I only write it down so I can hear it again. First the line is played. I listen for:
  - The beat, the pace, the rhythm.
  - The flow.

- The emphasis, or the lack of emphasis, or the relationship between what is emphasized and what isn't emphasized.
- The intensity, the caring, the mood, the feeling, the concern that is carried by the music of my language.

- I watch for the point of view, the angle of vision from which my language is making me see the subject, the distance I am standing from it. And, yes, my point of view does, in part, mean opinion. What do I think about the subject? What is my emotional attitude toward it?

- I am aware of what isn't appearing on the page that I expected to appear. It is always interesting what the line does not contain or does not point to, or is not interested in.

- I look to see what the line does include, with what it connects. The line is what makes the leaps we call thinking possible. The line is the leaping. It is the leap, it is the jump from one thing to another that gathers in from all our experience that leads us to discover what we did not know we knew. I try not to be frightened by what connects in a line, to accept what is brought up by my writing, whether I like the look of it or not.

- I pay attention to how I feel and if I am embarrassed or uncomfortable, if I have any strong feeling, I pay attention. The line connects as well as disconnects. It creates tension and challenge and contradiction.

- The line also produces analogy and examples and metaphor, especially metaphor. I pay close attention to metaphor.

- Alliteration. The line loves to lead by luring—watch out for alliteration. Don't let the reader see how helpful alliteration was in leading you on. Of course, being led on doesn't mean you end up where you should be.

- The wrong word is often as instructive as the right word, even more so sometimes, and typos are wonderful, and slips of the tongue and pen and word processor, errors, mistakes, are treasured, delighted in, studied.

It's marvelous when writing is pushed beyond meaning, beyond syntax, rule, and principle, when the whole business just breaks down. That's one of the nice things about the word processor for me. It allows me to write worse than I usually write so I can examine the mess and, perhaps, discover that language had, through failure, pushed things together in an interesting way.

> WHAT CAITLIN KNOWS
> at seven months
> standing wobble legged
> looking back over her shoulder
> woman already
>
> how fast she learns
> we say as she pursues
> on hands and knees
> the ball beyond the rug
>
> forgetting the knowing
> she brings from Death
>   Nothing
>   Dark
>   before
> she will live
> Caitlin will live
> learning what she knows
>
>
> WHAT CAITLIN KNOWS
> at seven months
> standing wobble legged
> glancing over her shoulder
> woman already
>
> how fast she learns
> we say as she fits

the yellow ring
over the red spike

forgetting the knowing
she brings from before
Caitlin will live
learning what she knows

In our desire to be responsible and to make our students write correctly there is a danger that they will misunderstand and think they have to write correctly from the beginning. But language will not be a tool of thinking unless our students are able to allow language to run free and stumble and fall. Caitlin turned from her proud parents standing by the couch and fell. Her father said, "She has to do a lot of falling." And writers have to do a lot of falling if they are to write anything worth reading.

Yes, I have students who don't seem to be able to write a sentence, and I seem to have more of them this semester. I have to work to make sure that when they finish their final drafts they have used the traditions of language to discipline their thinking and to make that thinking clear to others.

But I have other students who write too well too soon, and I have to help them—and I think I too often fail them—to get beyond their correctness, their teacher-induced, parent-induced, society-induced, genetic-induced desire to be correct, as if language could be contained by rules. The whole spectrum of students I work with—from remedial through graduate students to professional journalists—want correctness before meaning, before voice. And that can't be. If writers are to find the instructive line they must realize it is not only permissible to write badly, it is essential. We have to let language lead us to meaning. We have to write lines that may become sentences.

A call for research. We need to understand how writing can be made incorrect in a productive way. How do writers write badly to write well? What instructs them in their journal notes, in their mind before there are notes, and between the notes, in their early drafts, what allows them to see what we cannot see?

We have a vast inventory of drafts and notebook entries from writers living and dead that can help us in this research. But technology may be making that resource an endangered species, for on the video display terminal, bad writing is written (one of the values of the word processor is that it encourages productive bad writing) but then it is zapped and it flies to Saturn or beyond. Perhaps we can build research word processors that will save the bad writing—"Donate some of your k's to saving bad writing"—so interesting bad writing can be studied. If it is studied and understood, perhaps we can learn to teach our students to write badly so they can write well.

I have tried to do my part in this article, writing badly in a way that may be instructive to me, to you, to our students. My way of writing badly may not be yours or your students'. There is no one way to write badly any more than there is one way to write effectively. And remember that if this were written the way I usually write these days, most of what appears here would not appear, for I would have done what you may think I should have done and pushed the writer's favorite key: DELETE.

eleven

A Writer's Canon Revisited

<u>nulla dies sine linea</u> - never a day without a line.

The earlier the hour, the smugger the writer.

There will be no second draft without a first.

Be patient, listen quietly, the writing will come.

What do you do when it doesn't? Quit.

You have to write to discover what you have to say.

Listen. The voice of the writing will tell you what to do.

Write with information. The reader doesn't turn the page because of a hunger to applaud.

Every reader has a question which can't be avoided. Don't.

All writing is experimental. Failure is normal; success abnormal.

Hard work guarantees writing; nothing guarantees good writing.

The best writing is accidental. Writers are more accident prone than talkers.

Always remember: nobody asked you to be a writer.

Criticism angers; praise corrupts.

Doing is more important than the done.

Inspiration comes during writing.

Spontaneity comes during rewriting.

There will be no Tuesday morning without interruptions when you feel like writing.

Don't look back. Yes, the draft needs fixing. But first it needs writing.

twelve

Notes for Discussion

Paul Matsuda's Creative Nonfiction Class

<u>The three stupidist things I've done as a writer.</u>

1. Believed there was an aesthetic genre hierarchy: 1. Poetry, 2. Literary fiction, 3. Essay of literary criticism, 4. Drama, 5. Popular fiction, 6. Screenwriting, 7. Essay of personal experience, 8. Journalism. At age 77 I realized I am a storyteller who must tell the stories life has given me. The genre must come from the story to be told not the literary ambition of the writer.

2. Not finished drafts of books that could have been published because of lack of faith or deadline.

3. Took seriously the criticism or destructive praise of those who wanted me to write their poems, stories or books not my own.

<u>The three smartest things I've done as a writer.</u>

1. Tried to follow the advice of Horace -- nulla dies sine linea – and counted words. [Account sheet attached.]

2. Assigned specific tasks to my subconscious which kept writing during the 22 and1/2 hours I was away from the writing desk.

3. Established deadlines, then met them by breaking long projects into brief, achievable daily tasks.

<u>The four best pieces of writing advice I've been given.</u>

1. *I believe that the so-called "writing block" is a product of some kind of disproportion between your standards and your performance....one should lower his standards until there is no felt threshold to go over in writing. It's easy to write. You just shouldn't have standards that inhibit you from writing.....I can imagine a person beginning to feel he's not able to write up to that standard he imagines the world has set for him. But to me that's surrealistic. The only standard I can rationally have is the standard I'm meeting right now...You should be more willing to forgive yourself. It doesn't make any difference if you are good or bad today. The assessment of the product is something that happens after you've done it.* William Stafford

2. To write you have to set up a routine, to promise yourself that you will write. Just state in a loud voice that you will write so many pages a day, or write for so many hours a day. Keep the number of pages or hours within reason, and don't be upset if a day slips by. Start again; pick up the routine. Don't look for results. Just write, easily, quietly.
Janwilliam van de Wetering

3. Imagine yourself at your kitchen table, in your pajamas. Imagine one person you'd allow to see you that way, and write in the voice you'd use to that friend. Write about what makes you different.
Sandra Cisneros

4. We write about what we don't know about what we know.
Grace Paley

The three worst pieces of writing advice I've been given.

1. If you like it cut it out.

2. Know what you are going to say before you say it.

3. That's been said before.

The six most valuable tricks of my trade.

1. I don't start within an idea but a line or image with an unresolved tension.

2. I write for surprise, not what I know, but what I do not yet know.

3. I write out loud. My voice instructs.

4. I write fast to outrun the censor and cause the instructive failures necessary to effective writing.

5. I try to anticipate and answer the questions the reader will ask.

6. I revise by developing my strengths more than by correcting error.

thirteen

Internal Revision

A Process of Discovery
(*1978*)

Writing is rewriting. Most writers accept rewriting as a condition of their craft; it comes with the territory. It is not, however, seen as a burden but as an opportunity by many writers. Neil Simon points out, "Rewriting is when playwriting really gets to be fun. . . . In baseball you only get three swings and you're out. In rewriting, you get almost as many swings as you want and you know, sooner or later, you'll hit the ball."

Rewriting is the difference between the dilettante and the artist, the amateur and the professional, the unpublished and the published. William Gass testifies, "I work not by writing but rewriting." Dylan Thomas states, "Almost any poem is fifty to a hundred revisions—and that's after it's well along." Archibald MacLeish talks of "the endless discipline of writing and rewriting and rerewriting." Novelist Theodore Weesner tells his students at the University of New Hampshire his course title is not "Fiction Writing" but "Fiction Rewriting."

And yet rewriting is one of the writing skills least researched, least examined, least understood, and—usually—least taught. The vast majority of students, even those who take writing courses, get away with first-draft copy. They are never introduced to the opportunities of serious revision.

A search of the literature reveals relatively few articles or books on the rewriting process. I have a commonplace book which has grown from one thin journal to 24 3-inch-thick notebooks with more than 8,000 entries divided into prewriting, writing, and rewriting. Yet even with my interest in the process of rewriting— some of my colleagues would say my obsession—only four of those notebooks are labeled rewriting.

I suspect the term rewriting has, even for many writers, an aura of failure about it. Rewriting is too often taught as punishment, not as an opportunity for discovery or even as an inevitable part of the writing process. Most texts, in fact, confuse rewriting with editing, proofreading, or manuscript preparation. Yet rewriting almost always is the most exciting, satisfying part of the writing process.

The Writing Process

The most accurate definition of writing, I believe, is that it is the process of using language to discover meaning in experience and to communicate it. I believe this process can be described, understood and therefore learned. Prewriting, writing, and rewriting have been generally accepted as the three principal divisions of the writing process during the past decade. I would like to propose new terms for consideration, terms which may emphasize the essential process of discovery through writing: *prevision, vision,* and *revision.*

Of course, writing will, at times, seem to skip over one part of the writing process and linger on another, and the stages of the process also overlap. The writing process is too experimental and exploratory to be contained in a rigid definition; writers move back and forth through all stages of the writing process as they search for meaning and then attempt to clarify it. It is also true that most writers do not define, describe, or possibly even understand the writing process. There's no reason for them to know what they are doing if they do it well, any more than we need to know grammatical terms if we speak and write clearly. I am convinced, however, that most writers most of the time pass through the following distinct stages.

Prevision. This term encompasses everything that precedes the first draft—receptive experience, such as awareness (conscious and unconscious), observation, remembering; and exploratory experience, such as research, reading, interviewing, and note-taking. Writers practice the prevision skills of selecting, connecting, and evaluating significant bits of information provided by receptive and exploratory experience. Prevision includes, in my opinion, the underestimated skills of title and lead writing, which help the student identify a subject, limit it, develop a point of view towards it, and begin to find the voice to explore the subject.

Vision. In the second stage of the writing process, the first draft—what I call a discovery draft—is completed. This stage takes the shortest time for the writer—in many cases it is written at one sitting—but it is the fulcrum of the writing process. Before this first draft, which Peter Drucker calls "the zero draft," everything seems possible. By completing this vision of what may be said, the writer stakes out a territory to explore.

Revision. This is what the writer does after a draft is completed to understand and communicate what has begun to appear on the page. The writer reads to see what has been suggested, then confirms, alters, or develops it, usually through many drafts. Eventually a meaning is developed which can be communicated to a reader.

The Importance of Discovery

My main concern in this chapter is revision. But to be able to understand what I consider the most important task in the revision process, we have to appreciate the fact that writers much of the time don't know what they are going to write or even possibly what they have written. Writers use language as a tool of exploration to see beyond what they know. Most texts and most of our research literature have not accepted this concept or dealt with its implications.

Elie Wiesel says, "I write in order to understand as much as to be understood." The poet Tony Connor gives a recipe for writing a poem: "Invent a jungle and then explore it." William Stafford states, "You don't know what's going to happen. Nobody does." I have included at the end of this chapter forty-seven other quotations from my commonplace book which testify to the essential ignorance writers feel many times about what they are writing.

In teaching writing I often feel that the most significant step is made when a student enters into the writing process and experiences the discovery of meaning through writing. Yet this process of discovery has not been generally explored or understood for a number of reasons. First of all, it has not been experienced by nonwriters or admitted when it is experienced by writers in the less imaginative forms of writing. One professor of philosophy, after reading a text of mine, confessed he had been ashamed of the way he wrote, that he didn't know what to say or how to say it when he sat down to write. He had to write and write and write to find out what he had to say. He was embarrassed and didn't want his colleagues to know how dumb he was. When he read my book he found his activities were legitimate. I suspect such unjustified shame is more prevalent than we like to admit. Another professor told me recently that he makes assignments he could not complete by his own deadline. He explained, "My students are smarter than I am. I have to rewrite and rewrite many drafts." Yet he neither "confesses" this to his students nor allows them the opportunity to perform the writing task essential for them to achieve publication.

Most professors who are aware of the process of rewriting to discover meaning are uncomfortable thinking about it, to say nothing of discussing it in class. Discovery seems the province of the "creative writer," the writer who deals in poetry, fiction, or drama. Such activities are not quite respectable in the academic community, where we too often have a sex manual attitude: it's okay to read about it as long as you don't do it. But I am an academic schizophrenic, a "creative" writer and a "noncreative" writer. As the chairperson of a rather large department, I spend a good deal of my time writing memos to deans and vice provosts. (That's really creative writing.) I also moonlight occasionally as a corporate ghostwriter. I publish texts, novels, poems, and "papers." And in all of these roles I find the process of discovery through language taking place. I do not agree with the educational segregation of functional and imaginative writing, creative and noncreative writing. I know the process of discovery takes place when I write fiction and nonfiction, poetry and memos. To produce letters, reports, novels, essays, reviews, poems, and academic papers that say something, you have to allow language to lead you to meaning.

In drafting this paper I found myself writing, as I attempted to define the writing process, that the writer, after the first draft, is "not dealing with the vision but a fact." The word *vision* surprised me. It appeared on the page without premeditation. In reading it over I cut the sentence but decided the word was a better term than *writing* to describe the second stage of the writing process and, working from that point, saw the virtue of using the term *revision* for rewriting and then tried on the term *prevision* for size and found it fit, although I can't find it in my dictionary. I'm not sure that this is a discovery of enormous value, but it was fun; and I think this accident of language, this business of using words I didn't know I was going to use, has helped me understand the writing process a little bit better.

I suspect most of us have experienced many similar discoveries, but we feel it a failure: if we had a bit more IQ, we would have known the right word. I find few English teachers are comfortable with the concept of uncalculated discovery. They simply do not believe the testimony of writers when they say they write what they don't know, and this may indeed be an uncomfortable concept if you spend your classroom hours analyzing literature and telling your students exactly why the writer did what he or she did, as if literature resulted from the following of a detailed blueprint. Writing, fortunately for writers, is much more exciting than that. The writer does not plan but keeps adapting those plans to what is discovered on the page.

The writer, however, who lives in the academic community— and today most of us do—is surrounded by people who seem to know precisely what happens in a piece of literature. The other night my colleague, the poet Charles Simic, said his favorite poems were the ones he didn't understand, an unsettling confession in a department of English. It is hard to admit that you don't know what you're doing when you write. It seems a bit undignified, perhaps even cause for the removal of tenure. Surely my governor would think I ought to know what I'm doing when I sit down to write—I'm a full professor, for goodness sake—and yet I don't. And hope I never will.

Listening to a lecture the other day, I found myself doodling with language. (The better the lecture the more likely a piece of writing will start to happen on my notebook page.) From where I sat in the lecture hall, I could see an office door, and I watched a person in that office get up and shut the door against the lecture. It was an ordinary act, yet, for no reason I can recall, I found myself writing this on the page:

> I had an office at a university, an inside office, without window or air. The classrooms up and down the corridor would fill up with words until they spilled over and reached the edge of my half-opened door, a confident, almost arrogant mumble I could no longer bother to try to understand. Was I to be like the makers of those words, was I already like the students in my own Freshman sections? Perhaps the only good thing about this position was that Mother was dumbly proud and Father puzzled and angry, "Is this where they put you, an educated man? The union would kill me."
>
> If I hadn't killed a man, my life would have seemed trite. . . .

I have followed this short story for only a couple of pages in the past few days. I am ashamed to reveal the lines above—I don't know if they will lead me to a story—but I'm having fun and think I should share this experience, for it is revealing of the writing process. I did not intend to write a short story. I am working on a novel, a book of poems, and articles such as this one. Short fiction is not on the menu. I did not intend to write an academic short story. I do not like the genre. I do not particularly like the character who is appearing on my page, but I am interested in being within his head. I have not yet killed a man, to my knowledge, and I have never been a teaching assistant, although I have known many.

I want to repeat that there was absolutely no intent in what I was doing. The fact that the character had killed a person came as a total surprise to me. It seems too melodramatic, and I don't like this confessional voice, and I do not like the tense, and I have trouble dictating these words from my notebook to my wife, because they keep changing and leading me forward. I do not know if the killing was accidental or premeditated. I don't know the victim. I don't know the method. I don't know if it was imaginary. I do know the phrase "killed a man" appeared on the page. It may have come there because of what the father said; or, since in the next paragraph I discovered that the young man feels this one act gives him a certain distance from life, a sort of scenic overlook from which to view life, perhaps that idea came from the word *position* in the first paragraph. In my lower middle-class background, even a teaching assistant had a position, not a job. A little more of this kind of thing, however, and the story will never be written.

Writers must remain, to some degree, not only ignorant of what they are going to do but what they are doing. Mary Peterson just wrote me about her novel, "I need to write it before I can think about it, write it too fast for thought." Writers have to protect their ignorance, and it is not easy to remain ignorant, particularly in an English department. That may be one reason we have deemphasized the experience of discovery in writing.

Discovery, however, can be a frightening process. The terror of the empty page is real, because you simply do not know what you are going to say before you say it or if indeed you will have anything to say. I observe this process most dramatically at those times when I dictate early drafts of nonfiction to my wife, who types it on the typewriter. We have done this for years, and yet rather regularly she asks me to repeat what I have said or tell her what I am going to say so that she can punctuate. I don't think, after many books and many years, that she really believes me when I claim I can't remember what I've just said or that I don't know what I'm going to say next.

More so for analytical or academic writing

129

This process is even more frightening when you engage in the forms of writing that take you inside yourself. "There's not any more dangerous occupation in the world," says James Dickey of poetry. "The mortality rate is very, very high. Paul Valéry once said, 'one should never go into the self except armed to the teeth.' That's true. The kind of poets we're talking about—Berryman, Crane, Dylan Thomas—have created something against which they have no immunity and which they can not control."

Finally, many expert readers who teach English, and therefore writing, are ignorant of the process of discovery because it is not, and should not be, apparent in a finished work. After a building is finished, the flimsy scaffolding is taken away. Our profession's normal obsession with product rather than process leads us towards dangerous misconceptions about the writing process. I believe increasingly that the process of discovery, of using language to find out what you are going to say, is a key part of the writing process. In light of this I would like to reexamine the revision process.

The Two Principal Forms of Revision

The more I explore the revision process as a researcher and the more I experience it as a writer, the more convinced I am that there are two principal and quite separate editorial acts involved in revision.

Internal revision. Under this term, I include everything writers do to discover and develop what they have to say, beginning with the reading of a completed first draft. They read to discover where their content, form, language, and voice have led them. They use language, structure, and information to find out what they have to say or hope to say. The audience is one person: the writer.

External revision. This is what writers do to communicate what they have found they have written to another audience. It is editing and proofreading and much more. Writers now pay attention to the conventions of form and language, mechanics, and style. They eye their audience and may choose to appeal to it. They read as an outsider, and it is significant that such terms as *polish* are used by professionals: they dramatize the fact that the writer at this stage in the process may, appropriately, be concerned with exterior appearance.

Most writers spend more time, *much* more time, on internal revision than external revision. Yet most texts emphasize the least part of the process, the mechanical changes involved in the etiquette of writing, the superficial aspects of preparing a manuscript to be read, and pass over the process of internal revision. It's worth noting that it is unlikely intelligent choices in the editing process can be made unless writers thoroughly understand what they have said through internal revision.

Although I believe external revision has not been explored adequately or imaginatively, it has been explored. I shall concentrate on attempting to describe internal revision, suggesting opportunities for research, and indicating some implications for the teaching of writing.

The Process of Internal Revision

After the writer has completed the first draft, the writer moves toward the center of the writing process. E. M. Forster says, "The act of writing inspires me," and Valéry talks of "the inspiration of the writing desk." The writer may be closer to the scientist than to the critic at this point. Each piece of writing is an experiment. Robert Penn Warren says, "All writing that is any good is experimental: that is, it's a way of seeing what is possible."

Some pieces of writing come easily, without a great deal of internal revision. The experience is rare for most writers, however, and it usually comes after a lifetime of discipline, or sometimes after a long night of work, as it did when Robert Frost wrote "Stopping by Woods on a Snowy Evening." The important thing to understand is that the work that reads the most easily is often the product of what appears to be drudgery. Theodore Roethke wisely points out that "you will come to know how, by working slowly, to be spontaneous."

I have a relatively short 7-part poem of which there are 185 or more versions written over the past 2 years. I am no Roethke, but I have found it important to share with my students in my seminar on the teaching of writing a bit of the work which will never appear in public. I think they are impressed with how badly I write, with how many false starts and illiterate accidents it took for me to move forward towards some understanding of the climate in a tenement in which I lived as an only child, surrounded by a paralyzed grandmother and two rather childlike parents. The important thing for my students to see is that each word changed, each line crossed out, each space left on the page is an attempt to understand, to remember what I did not know I remembered.

During the process of internal revision, writers are not concerned with correctness in any exterior sense. They read what they have written so that they can deal with the questions of subject, of adequate information, of structure, of form, of language. They move from a revision of the entire piece down to the page, the paragraph, the sentence, the line, the phrase, the word. And then, because each word may give off an explosion of meaning, they move out from the word to the phrase, the line, the sentence, the paragraph, the page, the piece. Writers move in close and then move to visualize the entire piece. Again and again and again. As Donald Hall says, "The attitude to cultivate from the start is that revision is a way of life."

Discovery and Internal Revision

The concept of internal revision is new to me. This essay has given me the impetus to explore this area of the writing process. The further I explore the more tentative my conclusions. This chapter is, indeed, as I believe it was meant to be, a call for research, not a report of research. There are many things I do not understand as I experience and examine the process of internal revision. But in addition to my normal researches, I am part of a faculty which includes seven publishing writers, as well as many publishing scholars and critics. We share our work in process, and I have the advantage of seeing them discover what they have to say. I also see the work of graduate students in our writing program, many of whom are already publishing. And I watch the writing of students who are undergraduates at the university, in high school, in middle school, and in elementary school. And I think I can perceive four important aspects of discovery in the process of internal revision.

The first involves *content*. I think we forget that writers in all forms, even poetry, especially poetry, write with information. As English professors and linguistic researchers, we may concentrate on stylistic differences, forgetting that the writer engaged in the process of internal revision is looking through the word—or beyond the word or behind the word—for the information the word will symbolize. Sitting at a desk, pausing, staring out the window, the writer does not see some great thesaurus in the sky; the writer sees a character walking or hears a character speaking, sees a pattern of statistics which may lead toward a conclusion. Writers can't write nothing; they must have an abundance of information. During the process of internal revision, they gather new information or return to their inventory of information and draw on it. They discover what they have to say by relating pieces of specific information to other bits of information and use words to symbolize and connect that information.

This naturally leads to the discoveries related to *form and structure*. We all know Archibald MacLeish said that a poem should not mean but be, but what we do not always understand is that the being may be the meaning. Form is meaning, or a kind of meaning. The story that has a beginning, a middle, and an end implies that life has a beginning, a middle, and an end; exposition implies that things can be explained; argument implies the possibility of rational persuasion. As writers bring order to chaos, the order brings the writers toward meaning.

Third, *language* itself leads writer to meaning. During the process of internal revision (what some writers might call eternal revision), they reject words, choose new words, bring words together, switch their order around to discover what they are saying. "I work with language," says Bernard Malamud, "I love the flowers of afterthought."

Finally, I believe there is a fourth area, quite separate from content, form, or language, which is harder to define but may be as important as the other sources of discovery. That is what we call *voice.* I think voice, the way in which writers hear what they have to say, hear their point of view towards the subject, their authority, their distance from the subject, is an extremely significant form of internal revision.

We should realize that there may be fewer discoveries in form and voice as a writer repeats a subject or continues work in a genre which he or she has explored earlier and become proficient with. This lack of discovery—this excessive professionalism or slickness, the absence of discovery—is the greatest fear of mature, successful writers. They may know too much too early in the writing process.

Questions Looking for Questioners

Speculations about the writing process are fun to propose and entertaining to consider, but we will not understand the writing process unless we employ all of the methods and tools of modern research. Hypotheses suggested, such as the existence of an identifiable process of internal revision, must be subjected to tough, skeptical investigation. We must ask uncomfortable, demanding questions of the writing process. We will certainly not get the answers we expect—many of our pet theories will be destroyed—but the answers will bring new and better questions. Research into the writing process will eventually produce an understanding of how people write, which will have a profound effect on our educational procedures. We now attempt to teach a writing process we do not understand; research may allow us to teach what we understand.

The following are some of the questions researchers must ask:

1. How can the process of internal revision be described? The actual process of internal revision should be described in precise terms so we can understand the steps taken by a broad range of professional and student writers as they use language to discover and clarify the meaning of what they are writing. The process should be broken down and analyzed, defined and documented, so we can begin to understand what happens during internal revision.

2. What attitudes do effective writers bring to the task of internal revision? Attitude precedes and predetermines skill. Too often we attempt to teach skills and fail because we have not taught the attitudes which make the skill logical and obvious. It is important to know the attitude of effective revisors (or is it revisionists?) when they come to their own piece of writing. Do they accept the process of revision as a normal part of the writing process, or do they see it as punishment? Do writers expect their understanding of what they are saying to change as they write?

3. How do writers read their own copy? Writers perform a special, significant kind of reading when they read their own writing in process. Writers must achieve a detachment from their work that allows them to see what is on the page, not what they hoped will be on the page. They also must read with an eye to alternatives in content, form, structure, voice, and language. How do they read their own page and visualize the potential choices which may lead to a clarified meaning? How do they listen to the page to hear what is being said and what might be said?

4. What skills does the writer employ during the process of internal revision? There seem to be four distinct areas or types of internal revision. The first involves content, the collection and development of the raw material, the information with which the writer writes. The next is the form or structure of the writing itself. The last two are the voice and the language employed in the clarification of meaning. It is likely that there are overlapping but identifiable skills employed by the writer in each of these areas. The skills need to be observed and described. One unexplored skill which might help our understanding of internal revision is the writer's use of memory. There seem to be two significant forms of memory employed by the writer: one is the way in which writing unlocks information stored in the brain; the other is the memory of what the writer has previously written within the piece, which influences each choice during the process of internal revision. Another skill might come from

the fact some writers say they write with verbs, especially during the process of revision. It might be fruitful to examine how writers use verbs as the fulcrum of meaning.

5. What developmental stages are significant to an understanding of the process of internal revision? Applying our knowledge of how people react to their own world at different ages may help us understand the process of internal revision. There may be significant differences because of sex, levels of intelligence, or social-economic background. Our preconceptions about student willingness to revise may be wrong. Teachers who see rewriting as punishment may believe that students will not rewrite at certain levels of development and may, because of this conviction, discourage rewriting. In fact, their students may wish to revise, to explore the same subject in draft after draft, if they are given the opportunity. There may be a significant relationship between length and revision. Students may want to write longer than their teachers think they can, and the longer pieces students write may have a greater potential for exploration than shorter pieces. There are also indications that considerable familiarity with a subject, experience with a form, and confidence in a voice may increase discovery.

6. What new knowledge may help us understand the process of internal revision? There are significant new discoveries in brain research, for example, which may provide major breakthroughs in how writers write. The most significant article pointing out this new territory is Janet Emig's "The Biology of Writing: Another View of the Process" (1975). We also need to apply the latest findings of linguistic studies, rhetorical research, and learning theory to the process of internal revision. We must draw on as many fields as possible to attempt to understand the writing process. What can the teachers of foreign languages teach us? What can we learn from those who are studying the process of creativity in art, in music, in science? What can we learn from those who study the language of mathematics and from those

who design and use computers, which employ the language of mathematics to discover meaning in information?

7. What writing tools, habits, environments, or schedules influence the process of internal revision? Most writers scorn the interviewer's questions about what time of day they write and whether they use pen or typewriter. They feel this is trivia, and it may be, but it also may be significant trivia, for writers among themselves often seem obsessed by such matters. Writers are craftsmen who are greatly concerned with their tools—the texture, weight, size, and tint of paper; the flow of ink and its color; the design of the pen, its feel, and the breadth of its point. Most writers have superstitions about their favorite writing tools, and most of them vary their tools at different stages of the writing process. I write early drafts of poems in longhand (Mont Blanc fountain pen, thin point, permanent black ink, eye-ease green legal ruled paper), but in a stage central to the process of internal revision, I shift to a typewriter so I can see the poem in print. I find that most poets work in this way. Most writers also find certain environments, quiet or noisy, secluded or public, stimulate the writing process. (I hide in a secluded office these days, but I'd work best in a busy restaurant if I could afford to rent a table and if I could be anonymous—an impossibility in a small university town.) Writers usually are compulsive about the hour at which the work seems to go the best. (My present rule is at least 600 words before 9 a.m. every day.) Most writers seem to move towards the extremes of early morning or late at night, when they have the maximum energy or can work best without interruption, or can tap most easily into their subconscious. Writers have rituals or habits—reading or not reading what they have written or stopping in mid-sentence—which stimulate the flow of discovery through writing. These tricks of the trade may be important for students to know, and they may call for different learning styles or curriculum patterns than those normally imposed in school.

8. What subject areas, writing forms, or language patterns stimulate or discourage discovery of meaning through internal revision? We should observe writers at work on the traditionally most creative forms, such as poetry, but also on the less traditionally studied forms, such as technical writing, business letter writing, speech writing, news writing, and so on, to find out how these writers and the forms they use influence the process of discovery of meaning through language. The evidence we have is restricted to very few forms of writing. We need to extend this examination to all forms.

9. How do editors read writing and encourage improvements through the process of internal revision? Editors are highly specialized readers of writing in process who work closely with writers at each stage of the writing process. Yet, as far as I know, there have been no significant studies of how editors read copy, what they discover, and how they communicate with writers. This editing is not proofreading—it is the constructive examination of a draft with directions as to how further drafts may be developed. It should be obvious that editors are highly expert teachers and that they have a great deal to tell us about the writing process and the teaching of that process. They must motivate and employ techniques of communication which will make criticism constructive, which will stimulate, not discourage, improvement in writing. Their knowledge, attitudes, and skills might be a significant contribution to the understanding of the writing process and the means by which it can be taught.

10. What curricula, teaching environments, and methods encourage the improvement of writing through the process of internal revision? There are increasing numbers of teachers at every level, from preschool through graduate school, who are helping their students learn to write by taking them through the experience of the writing process. We need to observe these teachers at work and see exactly what their students do while they are engaged in the process of internal revision.

9

Those are just a few of the questions which should be asked of the process of internal revision. Each question will, of course, lead to additional questions. Each answer will produce even more questions, and researchers bringing their own special knowledge to the task will develop new questions. This is an exciting prospect, for the best and most obvious questions about the writing process have, amazingly, not been asked or investigated. We have a frontier ready for exploration.

How We Can Research Such Questions

I can suggest a number of ways to investigate the essential questions of internal revision:

Bring researchers in the writing process closer together with linguists, rhetoricians, and brain or neuroresearchers in teams and seminars to focus their divergent disciplines on an understanding of the writing process.

Examine writers' manuscripts to discover from the evidence on the page how writers read and revise to clarify their meaning for themselves.

Make use of accounts of the writing process—writers' interviews, diaries, journals, letters, autobiographies—to see what writers say they are doing.

Sponsor accounts of writers at work. Encourage writers to keep journals of an evolving piece of work, together with manuscript pages, so that they might become more aware and make others aware of the nature of their concern during the process of internal revision. (Many writers would refuse, of course, but some would not.)

Observe professional writers and editors at work, and interview them to see what they have done. Not many writers will stand still for this, but there may be some who would consent to be observed in a manner similar to the observation of students done by researchers such as Emig (1971) and Donald Graves (1975).

Collect and examine drafts of a number of versions of pieces of writing in many fields, not just examples of "creative writing" but examples of journalism, technical writing, scholarly writing. When I was an editor at *Time,* many copies of every single draft were typed, distributed, and I believe retained. A research project might collect and examine such drafts and perhaps interview the writers/editors who were producing them.

Observe students' writing and follow drafts evolving through the process of internal revision. Perhaps some students, for example, might be willing to read for revision or even revise using a scanner which shows how their eyes follow the text, where they stop and start.

Test the effectiveness of what we find out about the process of internal revision by having our students follow the examples of the writers who read and rewrite to discover what they have to say, and then see if the students' drafts define and refine a meaning more effectively than the early drafts.

These are just a few of the possible methods of researching internal revision. It seems clear, however, that the most productive method of exploring the writing process is the case study. We do not need extensive statistical surveys as much as we need close observation of a few writers and students doing the entire writing process by well-trained observers who follow their observations with intelligent, probing interviews. This method of investigation seems the one which will yield the basic data and concepts which will be tested and developed by other means of investigation.

The Implications for Teaching

If writers don't write what they know, but to learn what they may know, there may be significant implications for teaching, especially in the area of internal revision. Some of them are:

Stupid kids may not be stupid. Students classified as slow may simply have the illusion writers know what they are going to say before they say it. Since they do not know what they are

140

going to write, they may be paralyzed and not write. Such students, once they understand how writers write, may be released from this paralysis. Some slow students may then appear less slow when their writing evolves towards a subject.

Many articulate, verbal, glib students who are overrewarded for first-draft writing may be released from the prison of praise and high grades and encouraged to write much better than they ever have before.

Unmotivated students may be motivated to write when they find writing an adventure. In my teaching of "remedial" students, the exploration of a subject through many drafts is the single most significant motivating factor. Teachers constantly make the judgment that their least motivated students will not write many drafts, when in fact they are often the students who most quickly write many drafts once they experience the excitement of exploring a subject with language.

An understanding of the process of prevision, vision, and revision may result in the redesign of writing units so that students spend more time on prevision, far less time on vision, and much more time on revision. Students will have a greater opportunity in such units to discover an area they want to explore and more time to explore it.

Research into the writing process may reveal the process of writing to teachers so they will allow their students to experience it.

Finally, an understanding of the writing process may give literature teachers a new appreciation and understanding of the product we call literature. They may be able to read in a way which will help them discover the full implications of what the writer has done and is doing on the page.

Most of these implications could and should be evaluated by educational researchers. The teaching of writing certainly needs far more professional inquiry than the subjective accounts, anecdotes from the trenches, which so many of us, myself included, have produced in the past.

The new interest in the process of writing, rather than the product of writing, opens the door for important and interesting research which can employ all of the tools of the intelligent investigation. It is a job which needs to be done. The process of writing—of using language to discover meaning and communicate it—is a significant human act. The better we understand how people write—how people think—the better we may be able to write and to teach writing.

Appendix: Writers on Prevision, Vision, and Revision

Edward Albee: Writing has got to be an act of discovery. . . . I write to find out what I'm thinking about.

W. H. Auden: Language is the mother, not the handmaiden, of thought; words will tell you things you never thought or felt before.

James Baldwin: You go into a book and you're in the dark, really. You go in with a certain fear and trembling. You know one thing. You know you will not be the same person when this voyage is over. But you don't know what's going to happen to you between getting on the boat and stepping off.

Robert Bolt: Writing a play is thinking, not thinking about thinking.

Truman Capote: If there is no mystery, for the artist, to solve inside of his art, then there's no point in it. . . . For me, every act of art is the act of solving a mystery.

Frank Conroy: Most often I come to an understanding of what I am writing about as I write it (like the lady who doesn't know what she thinks until she says it).

John Dos Passos: Curiosity urges you on—the driving force.

Alan Dugan. When I'm successful, I find the poem will come out saying something that I didn't know, believe, or had intellectually agreed with.

Robert Duncan: If I write what you know, I bore you; if I write what I know, I bore myself; therefore I write what I don't know.

William Faulkner: It begins with a character, usually, and once he stands up on his feet and begins to move, all I do is trot along behind him with a paper and pencil trying to keep up long enough to put down what he says and does.

Gabriel Fielding: Writing to me is a voyage, an odyssey, a discovery, because I'm never certain of precisely what I will find.

E. M. Forster: How do I know what I think until I see what I say?

Robert Frost: For me the initial delight is in the surprise of remembering something I didn't know I knew. . . . I have never started a poem yet whose end I knew. Writing a poem is discovering.

Christopher Fry: My trouble is I'm the sort of writer who only finds out what he's getting at by the time he's got to the end of it.

Rumer Godden: Of course one never knows in draft if it's going to turn out, even with my age and experience.

Joanne Greenberg: Your writing is trying to tell you something. Just lend an ear.

Graham Greene: The novel is an unknown man and I have to find him. . . .

Nancy Hale: Many an author will speak of writing, in his best work, more than he actually knows.

Robert Hoyden: As you continue writing and rewriting, you begin to see possibilities you hadn't seen before. Writing a poem is always a process of discovery.

Shirley Hazzard: I think that one is constantly startled by the things that appear before you on the page when you're writing.

George V. Higgins: I have no idea what I'll say when I start a novel. I work fast so I can see how it will come out.

Cecelia Holland: One of the reasons a writer writes, I think, is that his stories reveal so much he never thought he knew.

William Inge: I don't start a novel or a play saying, "I'll write about such and such." I start with an idea and then find out what I'm writing about.

Galway Kinnell: I start off but I don't know where I'm going; I try this avenue and that avenue, that turns out to be a dead end, this is a dead end, and so on. The search takes a long time and I have to back-track often.

Stanley Kunitz: For me the poem is always something to be discovered.

Margaret Laurence: Each novel is a kind of voyage of discovery.

Denise Levertov: Writing poetry is a process of discovery. . . . You can smell the poem before you see it. . . . Like some animal.

C. Day Lewis: First, I do not sit down at my desk to put into verse something that is already clear in my mind. If it were clear in my mind, I should have no incentive or need to write about it. . . . We do not write in order to be understood; we write in order to understand.

Bernard Malamud: A writer has to surprise himself to be worth reading.

William Matthews: The easiest way for me to lose interest is to know too much of what I want to say before I begin.

Mary McCarthy: Every short story, at least for me, is a little act of discovery. A cluster of details presents itself to my scrutiny, like a mystery that I will understand in the course of writing or sometimes not fully until afterward . . . a story that you do not learn something from while you are writing it, that does not illuminate something for you, is dead, finished before you started it.

Arthur Miller: I'm discovering it, making up my own story. I think at the typewriter.

Henry Miller: Writing, like life itself, is a voyage of discovery.

Alberto Moravia: One writes a novel in order to know why one writes it.

Wright Morris: The language leads, and we continue to follow where it leads.

144

Flannery O'Connor: The only way, I think, to learn to write short stories is to write them, and then try to discover what you have done.

Lawrence Osgood: Writing is like exploring . . . as an explorer makes maps of the country he has explored.

Jules Renard: The impulse of the pen. Left alone, thought goes as it will. As it follows the pen, it loses its freedom. It wants to go one way, the pen another. It is like a blind man led astray by his cane, and what I came to write is no longer what I wished to write.

Adrienne Rich: Poems are like dreams; you put into them what you don't know you know.

Charles Simic: You never know when you begin a poem what it has in store for you.

William Stafford: I don't see writing as a communication of something already discovered, as "truths" already known. Rather, I see writing as a job of experiment. It's like any discovery job; you don't know what's going to happen until you try it.

Mark Strand: What I want to do in a poem is discover what it is that I have to say.

John Updike: Writing and rewriting are a constant search for what one is saying.

Kurt Vonnegut: It's like watching a teletype machine in a newspaper office to see what comes out.

David Wagoner: For me, writing poetry is a series of bewildering discoveries, a search for something that remains largely unknown even when you find it.

Robert Penn Warren: A poem is an exploration not a working out of a theme.

Thomas Williams: A writer keeps surprising himself . . . he doesn't know what he is saying until he sees it on the page.

fourteen

Don—Still the Copy Editor

ONE WRITER'S NOTES

Donald M. Murray

The word processor makes [hides] the craft of editing, easier - but and invisible. The skills of cutting, adding, moving, with all their infinite variations, are done [accomplished] in electronic secrecy while by machine, and the text remains ever [for] virginal and young, never showing the scars of its evolution.

Sometimes I wonder if the electronic process [computer makes editing] is too easy. It seems [editing becomes so] anticeptic and remote, and [that] I feel nostalgic for the days of a more intimate relationship [with my texts]. Crossed out lines, some with dots under them to restore them to life, words inserted above and below lines, other words transposed with a special weaving line, sentences and paragraphs circled and moved by arrow, chunks of text slashed out, all the evidence of the writer at work. I can feel the scissors in my hand cutting the text, into new order and the smell of the glue, or [heal] the (click of staple) as [into place] pieces of text are forced together. I used to love [loved] the grand messiness of my creations.

I am nostalgic, but I won't return. The computer is easier. But I wonder [worry] if [that] writers who have not edited by hand, cut and pasted, will know [learn] the same craft I have [earlier] learned in another time [generation].

***

The final satisfaction for the writer is not publication, that long after the fact anticlimax, but the final editing when the writer practices the craft of precision, interacting [interacts] with the text so that it is [becomes] accurate, clear, and so natural it appears spontaneous. Here is the joy of working within language, shaping, fitting, joining - cabinetmaking.

- 1 -

Every morning between 9 and 12 I go to my room and sit before a piece of paper. Many times I just sit for three hours with no ideas coming to me. But I know one thing: If an idea does come between 9 and 12, I am there ready for it. – *Flannery O'Connor*

If I don't sit down practically immediately after breakfast, I won't sit down all day. – *Graham Greene*

To be a writer is to sit down at one's desk in the chill portion of every day, and to write. – *John Hersey*

Two simple rules: a) You don't have to write. b) You can't do anything else. – *Raymond Chandler*

The writing generates the writing. – *E. L. Doctorow*

There is no one right way. Each of us finds a way that works for him. But there is a wrong way. The wrong way is to finish your writing day with no more words on paper than when you began. Writers write. – *Robert B. Parker*

A day in which I don't write leaves a taste of ashes.
　　　　　　– *Simone de Beauvoir*

If you keep working, inspiration comes. – *Alexander Calder*

To write you have to set up a routine, to promise yourself that you will write. Just state in a loud voice that you will write so many pages a day, or write for so many hours a day. Keep the number of pages or hours within reason, and don't be upset if a day slips by. Start again, pick up the routine. Don't look for results. Just write, easily, quietly. – *Janwillem van de Wetering*

Perfect is the enemy of good. – *John Jerome*

fifteen

The Listening Eye

Reflections on the Writing Conference
(1979)

It was dark when I arrived at my office this winter morning, and it is dark again as I wait for my last writing student to step out of the shadows in the corridor for my last conference. I am tired, but it is a good tired, for my students have generated energy as well as absorbed it. I've learned something of what it is to be a childhood diabetic, to raise oxen, to work across from your father at 115 degrees in a steel-drum factory, to be a welfare mother with three children, to build a bluebird trail, to cruise the disco scene, to be a teen-age alcoholic, to salvage World War II wreckage under the Atlantic, to teach invented spelling to first graders, to bring your father home to die of cancer. I have been instructed in other lives, heard the voices of my students they had not heard before, shared their satisfaction in solving the problems of writing with clarity and grace. I sit quietly in the late afternoon waiting to hear what Andrea, my next student, will say about what she accomplished on her last draft and what she intends on her next draft.

It is nine weeks into the course and I know Andrea well. She will arrive in a confusion of scarves, sweaters and canvas bags, and then produce a clipboard from which she will precisely read exactly what she has done and exactly what she will do. I am an observer of her own learning, and I am eager to hear what she will tell me.

I am surprised at this eagerness. I am embedded in tenure, undeniably middle-aged, one of the gray, fading professors I feared I would become, but still have not felt the bitterness I saw in many of my own professors and see in some of my colleagues. I wonder if I've missed something important, if I'm becoming one of those aging juveniles who bound across the campus from concert to lecture, pleasantly silly.

There must be something wrong with a fifty-four-year-old man who is looking forward to his thirty-fifth conference of the day. It is twelve years since I really started teaching by conference. I average seventy-five conferences a week, thirty weeks a year, then there's summer teaching and workshop teaching of teachers. I've probably held far more than 30,000 writing conferences, and I am still fascinated by this strange, exposed kind of teaching, one on one.

It doesn't seem possible to be an English teacher without the anxiety that I will be exposed by my colleagues. They will find out how little I do; my students will expose me to them; the English Department will line up in military formation in front of Hamilton Smith Hall and, after the buttons are cut off my Pendleton shirt, my university library card will be torn once across each way and let flutter to the ground.

The other day I found myself confessing to a friend, "Each year I teach less and less, and my students seem to learn more. I guess what I've learned to do is to stay out of their way and not to interfere with their learning."

I can still remember my shock years ago when I was summoned by a secretary from my classroom during a writing workshop. I had labored hard but provoked little discussion. I was angry at the lack of student involvement and I was angry at the summons to the department office. I stomped back to the classroom and was almost in my chair before I realized the classroom was full of talk about the student papers. My students were not even aware I had returned. I moved back out to the corridor, feeling rejected, and let the class teach itself.

Of course, that doesn't always happen, and you have to establish the climate, the structure, the attitude. I know all that, and yet . . .

I used to mark up every student paper diligently. How much I hoped my colleagues would see how carefully I marked up student papers. I alone held the bridge against the pagan hordes. No one escaped the blow of my "awk." And then one Sunday afternoon a devil bounded to the arm of my chair. I started giving purposefully bad counsel on my students' papers to see what would happen. "Do this backward," "add adjectives and adverbs," "be general and abstract," "edit with a purple pencil," "you don't mean black you mean white." Not one student questioned my comments.

I was frightened my students would pay so much attention to me. They took me far more seriously than I took myself. I remembered a friend in advertising told me about a head copywriter who accepted a piece of work from his staff and held it overnight without reading it. The next day he called in the staff and growled, "Is this the best you can do?"

They hurried to explain that if they had more time they could have done better. He gave them more time. And when they met the new deadline, he held their copy again without reading it, and called them together again and said, "Is *this* the best you can do?"

Again they said if only they had more time, they could . . . He gave them a new deadline. Again he held their draft without reading. Again he gave it back to them. Now they were angry. They said, yes, it was the best they could do and he answered, "I'll read it."

I gave my students back their papers, unmarked, and said, make them better. And they did. That isn't exactly the way I teach now, not quite, but I did learn something about teaching writing.

In another two-semester writing course I gave 220 hours of lecture during the year. My teaching evaluations were good; students signed up to take this course in advance. Apparently I was well-prepared, organized, entertaining. No one slept in my class, at least with their eyes shut, and they did well on the final exam. But that devil found me in late August working over my lecture notes and so, on the first day of class, I gave the same final exam I had given at the end of the year. My students did better before the 220 hours of lectures than my students had done afterwards. I began to learn something about teaching a non-content writing course, about under-teaching, about not teaching what my students already know.

The other day a graduate student who wanted to teach writing in a course I supervise indicated, "I have no time for non-directive teaching. I know what my students need to know. I know the problems they will have—and I teach them."

I was startled, for I do not know what my students will be able to do until they write without any instructions from me. Rut he had a good reputation, and I read his teaching evaluations. The students liked him, but there was a minor note of discomfort. "He does a good job of teaching, but I wish he would not just teach me what I already know" and "I wish he would listen better to what we need to know." But they liked him. They could understand what he wanted, and they could give it to him. I'm uncomfortable when my students are uncomfortable, but more uncomfortable when they are comfortable.

I teach the student not the paper but this doesn't mean I'm a "like wow" teacher. I am critical and I certainly can be directive but I listen before I speak. Most times my students make tough— sometimes too tough—evaluations of their work. I have to curb their too critical eye and help them see what works and what might work so they know how to read evolving writing so it will evolve into writing worth reading.

I think I've begun to learn the right questions to ask at the beginning of a writing conference.

"What did you learn from this piece of writing?"
"What do you intend to do in the next draft?"
"What surprised you in the draft?"
"Where is the piece of writing taking you?"
"What do you like best in the piece of writing?"
"What questions do you have of me?"

I feel as if I have been searching for years for the right questions, questions which would establish a tone of master and apprentice, no, the voice of a fellow craftsman having a conversation about a piece of work, writer to writer, neither praise nor criticism but questions which imply further drafts, questions which draw helpful comments out of the student writer.

And now that I have my questions, they quickly become unnecessary. My students ask these questions of themselves before they come to me. They have taken my conferences away from me. They come in and tell me what has gone well, what has gone wrong, and what they intend to do about it.

Some of them drive an hour or more for a conference that is over in fifteen minutes. It is pleasant and interesting to me, but don't they feel cheated? I'm embarrassed that they tell me what I would hope I would tell them, but probably not as well. My students assure me it is important for them to prepare themselves for the conference and to hear what I have to say.

"But I don't say anything," I confess. "You say it all."

They smile and nod as if I know better than that, but I don't.

What am I teaching? At first I answered in terms of form: argument, narrative, description. I never said comparison and contrast, but I was almost as bad as that. And then I grew to answering, "the process." "I teach the writing process." "I hope my students have the experience of the writing process." I hear my voice coming back from the empty rooms which have held teacher workshops.

That's true, but there's been a change recently. I'm really teaching my students to react to their own work in such a way that they write increasingly effective drafts. They write; they read what they've written; they talk to me about what they've read and what the reading has told them they should do. I nod and smile and put my feet up on the desk, or down on the floor, and listen and stand up when the conference runs too long. And I get paid for this?

Of course, what my students are doing, if they've learned how to ask the right questions, is write oral rehearsal drafts in conference. They tell me what they are going to write in the next draft, and they hear their own voices telling me. I listen and they learn.

But I thought a teacher had to talk. I feel guilty when I do nothing but listen. I confess my fear that I'm too easy, that I have too low standards, to a colleague, Don Graves. He assures me I am a demanding teacher, for I see more in my students than they do—to their surprise, not mine.

I hear voices from my students they have never heard from themselves. I find they are authorities on subjects they think ordinary. I find that even my remedial students write like writers, putting down writing that doesn't quite make sense, reading it to see what sense there might be in it, trying to make sense of it, and—draft after draft—making sense of it. They follow language to see where it will lead them, and I follow them following language.

It is a matter of faith, faith that my students have something to say and a language in which to say it. Sometimes I lose that faith but if I regain it and do not interfere, my students do write and I begin to hear things that need saying said well.

This year, more than ever before, I realize I'm teaching my students what they've just learned.

They experiment, and when the experiment works I say, "See, look what happened." I put the experiment in the context of the writing process. They brainstorm, and I tell them that they've brainstormed. They write a discovery draft, and I point out that many writers have to do that. They revise, and then I teach them revision.

When I boxed I was a counterpuncher. And I guess that's what I'm doing now, circling my students, waiting, trying to shut up—it isn't easy—trying not to interfere with their learning, waiting until they've learned something so I can show them what they've learned. There is no text in my course until my students write. I have to study the new text they write each semester.

It isn't always an easy text to read. The student has to decode the writing teacher's text; the writing teacher has to decode the student's writing. The writing teacher has to read what hasn't been written yet. The writing teacher has the excitement of reading unfinished writing.

Those papers without my teacherly comments written on them haunt me. I can't escape the paranoia of my profession. Perhaps I should mark up their pages. There are misspellings, comma splices, sentence fragments (even if they are now sanctified as "English minor sentences"). Worse still, I get papers that have no subject, no focus, no structure, papers that are undeveloped and papers that are voiceless.

I am a professional writer—a hired pen who ghostwrites and edits—yet I do not know how to correct most student papers. How do I change the language when the student writer doesn't yet know what to say? How do I punctuate when it is not clear what the student must emphasize? How do I question the diction when the writer doesn't know the paper's audience?

The greatest compliment I can give a student is to mark up a paper. But I can only mark up the best drafts. You can't go to work on a piece of writing until it is near the end of the process, until the author has found something important to say and a way to say it. Then it may be clarified through a demonstration of professional editing.

The student sits at my right hand and I work over a few paragraphs, suggesting this change, that possibility, always trying to show two, or three, or four alternatives so that the student makes the final choice. It is such satisfying play to mess around with someone else's prose that it is hard for me to stop. My best students snatch their papers away from my too eager pen but too many allow me to mess with their work as if I knew their world, their language, and what they had to say about their world in their language. I stop editing when I see they really appreciate it. It is not my piece of writing; it is not my mind's eye that is looking at the subject; not my language which is telling what the eye has seen. I must be responsible and not do work which belongs to my students, no matter how much fun it is. When I write it must be my own writing, not my students'.

I realize I not only teach the writing process, I follow it in my conferences. In the early conferences, the prewriting conferences, I go to my students; I ask questions about their subject, or if they don't have a subject, about their lives. What do they know that I don't know? What are they authorities on? What would they like to know? What would they like to explore? I probably lean forward in these conferences; I'm friendly, interested in them as individuals, as people who may have something to say.

Then, as their drafts begin to develop and as they find the need for focus, for shape, for form, I'm a bit removed, a fellow writer who shares his own writing problems, his own search for meaning and form.

Finally, as the meaning begins to be found, I lean back, I'm more the reader, more interested in the language, in clarity. I have begun to detach myself from the writer and from the piece of writing which is telling the student how to write it. We become fascinated by this detachment which is forced on us as a piece of writing discovers its own purpose.

After the paper is finished and the student starts on another, we go back through the process again and I'm amused to feel myself leaning forward, looking for a subject with my student. I'm not coy. If I know something I think will help the student, I share it. But I listen first—and listen hard (appearing casual)—to hear what my student needs to know.

Now that I've been a teacher this long I'm beginning to learn how to be a student. My students are teaching me their subjects. Sometimes I feel as if they are paying for an education and I'm the one getting the education. I learn so many things. What it feels like to have a baby, how to ski across a frozen lake, what rights I have to private shoreline, how complex it is to find the right nursery school when you're a single parent with three children under six years old.

I expected to learn of other worlds from my students but I didn't expect—an experienced (old) professional writer—to learn about the writing process from my students. But I do. The content is theirs but so is the experience of writing—the process through which they discover their meaning. My students are writers and they teach me writing most of the time.

I notice my writing bag and a twenty-page paper I have tossed towards it. Jim has no idea what is right or wrong with the paper—and neither do I. I've listened to him in conference and I'm as confused as he is. Tomorrow morning I will do my writing, putting down my own manuscript pages, then, when I'm fresh from my own language, I will look at Jim's paper. And when he comes back I will have at least some new questions for him. I might even have an answer, but if I do I'll be suspicious. I am too fond of answers, of lists, of neatness, of precision; I have to fight the tendency to think I know the subject I teach. I have to wait for each student draft with a learning, listening eye. Jim will have re-read the paper and thought about it too and I will have to be sure I listen to him first, for it is his paper, not mine.

Andrea bustles in, late, confused, appearing disorganized. Her hair is totally undecided; she wears a dress skirt, lumberjack boots, a fur coat, a military cap. She carries no handbag, but a canvas bag bulging with paper as well as a lawyer's briefcase which probably holds cheese and bread.

Out comes the clipboard when I pass her paper back to her. She tells me exactly what she attempted to do, precisely where she succeeded and how, then informs me what she intends to do next. She will not work on this draft; she is bored with it. She will go back to an earlier piece, the one I liked and she didn't like. Now she knows what to do with it. She starts to pack up and leave.

I smile and feel silly; I ought to do something. She's paying her own way through school. I have to say something.

"I'm sorry you had to come all the way over here this late."

Andrea looks up surprised. "Why?"

"I haven't taught you anything."

"The hell you haven't. I'm learning in this course, really learning."

I start to ask Andrea what she's learning but she's out the door and gone. I laugh, pack up my papers, and walk home.

sixteen

Don Drawing Don
(1981)

If you asked Don to sign a book, he'd often add a caricature of himself—beard and belly—to the words. Here's one of himself teaching.

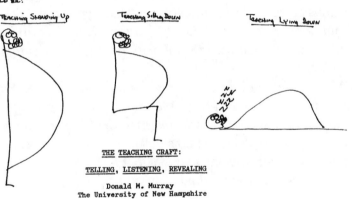

English Education

ANNE — I cut off its tail.

SHOULD BE:

TEACHING STANDING UP   Teaching Sitting Down   Teaching Lying Down

THE TEACHING CRAFT:

TELLING, LISTENING, REVEALING

Donald M. Murray
The University of New Hampshire

The mirror surprises. The gray beard has turned white. The apprentice teacher is asked to speak as a master. The amateur who came to teaching late teaches teachers, and what was chutzpah is confirmed by rank. I have fooled them all.

But not myself. I am still apprentice to two trades which can not be learned: writing and teaching. I am thankful for the anxiety of each blank page, the stagefright before each new class.

I spend my time looking ahead to what I have not tried, to what I have not learned. But when I am asked to look back over my

---

This article was adapted by the author from his CEE Luncheon Address, November 21, 1981, at the NCTE Convention in Boston.

seventeen

One Writer's Secrets
(1986)

Arriving as a professional writer in the academic world, I was astonished at the importance of publishing to the careers of young academics and even more astonished by their total lack of training for publication. People would talk more easily—often too easily— about their intimate fears and parental drinking customs than how they wrote.

I proposed to the editor of College Composition and Communication, *Richard Larson, that he devote an issue to the practical questions of scholarly life, possibly tied into a special session at the annual convention. That didn't work out, but this article was invited and published after some very wise editorial suggestions from Larson.*

I was very much aware of my own eccentricity—a bustling duckling among swans. I was far from the normal academic, and I hoped that my confessions would inspire others whose counsel might be more helpful to young scholars and researchers. I haven't seen a flood of such helpful material, but I hope that my article has been helpful to a few graduate students or beginning assistant professors.

And I hope that this look backstage at a writer who has been considered "productive" will strip away the mystery and help more teachers write.

D. M.

It is good form in English department offices and corridors to grump, grouse, growl, even whine about how the writing is going. Such labor, such a dreary business, how grubby, how ridiculous to expect publication, as if an article could reveal the subtleties of a finely tuned mind. The more you publish, the more tactful it is to moan and groan. The danger is that young colleagues, new to the academy, may believe us. They may think we who publish are performing penance, obediently fulfilling a vow to publish out of fear of perishing, when this academic and others will slyly look around to see who is listening, then confess, "writing is fun."

The focus is on writing. That is where writers discover they know more than they knew they knew, where accidents of diction or syntax reveal meaning, where sentences run ahead to expose a thought. If the writing is done, publication—perhaps not this piece but the next or the one after that—will follow. And publishing promises a lifetime of exploration and learning, active membership in a scholarly community, and the opportunity for composition teachers to practice what we preach.

I will share some of the methods that have helped me publish what some would say—and have said—is an excessive number of articles and books on the composing process. I do not do this to suggest that others should work as I work, but as a way to invite others who publish to reveal their own craft so those who join our profession can become productive members of it—and share the secret pleasure in writing which we feel but rarely admit.

Attitudes That Allow Writing

Our attitudes usually predict and limit our accomplishments. I find that I have to encourage, model, and continually relearn certain attitudes if I want my students to write—and if I want myself to write.

- No publication is the final theological word on a subject. Too many academics believe they have to write *the* article or book on their topic. That is impossible. Each publication is merely a contribution to a continuous professional conversation. I was paralyzed by the idea I had to deliver the Truth—Moses-like; I began to write when I realized all I had to do was speculate, question, argue, create a model, take a position, define a problem, make an observation, propose a solution, illuminate a possibility to participate in a written conversation with my peers. There is an increasing emphasis on research, but still it is not necessary to wait to report on the ultimate, all-inclusive research project.

- There is no need to be consistent. Learning does not stop with publication. I continue to learn from my students, my colleagues, my reading, my observations, my researches, my teaching, and my writing. I learn from each draft. Change is essential to learning. Of course, I will contradict myself from time to time.

- Ask your own questions and find your own answers. Few people talked about the writing process when I started publishing in this field. No matter, it was what interested me. I didn't think my articles would get published, but I sent them off, and most of them were.

- Use the mail. My articles, poems, and short stories that don't get into the mail never get published. Submit. Maybe you'll find an editor who is suffering empty journal terror. We like to believe that all acceptances are rational and all rejections irrational. I've learned from participating on both sides of the process that acceptances are often as irrational as rejections.

- Start at the top. Maybe the best journals will not publish my stuff, but at least they've had their chance.

- Remember what Al Pacino said: "Forget the career and do the work." The doing is far more satisfying than the done. The discoveries made during the writing—the thinking process—are far more exciting than receiving half a dozen copies of a journal with your article in it a year or two later.

- If it isn't fun, don't do it. The lack of fun will show. Since both acceptance and rejection are irrational, you might as well have the satisfaction of doing what you want to do. We are lucky to have a vocation of scholarship, a calling. But who is calling? Ourselves. We are all self-appointed authorities. If our work is not our play, then we should quit, take a job, and make some real money.

Some Tricks of the Academic Trade

As you develop the attitudes that will allow you to publish, then you may be able to develop techniques and strategies that help get the work done. Some tricks of my trade are:

- Keep a planning notebook with you to play in at the office, at home, in the car, on the airplane, at faculty meetings (especially at faculty meetings), while you're watching television, sitting in a parking lot, or eating a lonely lunch. Such play has allowed me to write on the advantages of writer's block, to catch a glimpse of ideas about planning and vision, which have become talks, articles, and sections of my books. I pay most attention to the questions that keep reoccurring, the connections that surprise me, the patterns that give the familiar an interesting unfamiliarity.

    The notebook, which I call a daybook, will make it possible for you to use fragments of time, and fragments of time are all that most of us really have. Fifteen minutes, ten, five, two, one, less. In this book you can make lists, notes, diagrams, collect the quotes and citations, paste in key articles and references, sketch outlines, draft titles, leads, endings, key paragraphs that will make it possible for you to be ready to write when you have an hour, or two, or three clear.

- Write daily. I try to follow the counsel of Horace, Pliny, Trollope, Updike: *nulla dies sine linea*—never a day without a line—but a line for me does not mean a polished sentence of finished prose. It means the daily habit of talking to myself in writing, playing with ideas, letting a piece of writing grow and ripen until it is ready to be written. It is intellectual play, self-indulgent, introspective, and immensely satisfying. Each time I play with an idea I purposely do not look back at my previous notes. Then, after I finish the daily entry, I look back to see what I'd said on the same subject before and add ideas that seem worth adding.

In this way I keep turning over the compost of my thoughts and discover what I didn't know I knew.

The academic schedule encourages the illusion that you can get your writing done on the day free from teaching, during the semester with a lower teaching load, between semesters, next summer, or on sabbatical. Nonsense. When those times come you can't suddenly take up an alien craft. The productive scholar is in the habit of writing, at least notes, at least lists, at least fragmentary drafts, at least something that keeps the topic alive and growing so that writing will come that is ready to be written.

If I have a good title; a well-honed first sentence, paragraph, or page; a hint of the ending; a list of three to five points that will lead me toward that end, I can put a draft on hold, for weeks, if necessary, and not lose the freshness of the first draft that will follow.

- Pick the best time for your writing and try to protect that time. Be selfish. Writing is the best preparation for teaching. I schedule my teaching in the afternoon, which is my normal slump period. In the afternoon I respond to the stimulus of the class, the conference, or the meeting. But only in the morning do I respond to the stimulus of the blank page.

My most difficult problem is to keep the moat around my writing time filled with alligators and absolutely terrifying snakes. I do not spring out of bed ready and eager to write. I need time I can waste in which my subconscious can prepare itself for the period at the writing desk. And I need time on the other end of the writing period. If I start to write too close to when I have to be at school, the demands of teaching invade my mind and I cannot concentrate on the writing task. Bernard Malamud described this too rare concentration best when he said, "If it is winter in the book, spring surprises me when I look up." Concentration is not only important for the work but to the mental health of the worker. My agent did not want me to accept a teaching job. I think she said it would be like "being bitten to death by ducks." I didn't know how wise she was. It was far easier to achieve concentration in the confusion of the city room on deadline than in the distracting, fragmented academic world. Wasn't it Mencken who said, "Campus politics are so vicious because the stakes are so low"? The hardest thing I do is to find time, to sit, to wait, to listen for writing.

- Read widely as well as deeply; read writing as well as writing about writing. Our training teaches us to read critically and narrowly, and it is vital to probe deeply into a specialty or a text. The best ideas, however, come from connecting information from different disciplines. We should also be bottom-feeders, gobbling up everything that comes our way—reading a book on science, a line of poetry, a newspaper story, a picture in a museum, a question by a student, a move by a hockey player, a pattern of music, a comment overheard in an elevator, the look on a face seen from a bus window, reading our world in such a way that our scholarly work is fed by connections from the world, so that the work we do is in context. If it is fed by the world, it may, if we are effective, return to feed the world.

- Keep a list of questions to which you want to seek answers, answers for which you wish to form questions, territories of fascinating ignorance you wish to explore. How do writers choose and use test readers? How does thinking style affect writing process? How does a writing task change process? Does MTV have a positive influence on the writing or reading process? How do good student writers read their evolving drafts? Keep moving around, and don't be trapped in your own specialty. Some people took my work on revision more seriously than I took it myself, and I consciously moved toward studying prewriting. Use your list to turn class presentations, invitations to give talks and workshops, opportunities to publish articles or chapters or books to your own advantage. Set your own agenda, so that each year you sniff along two or three new trails of thought.

- Put yourself on the spot. Accept teaching, speaking, and writing assignments that are just beyond reach—but within reach. Join local, regional, and national organizations within our discipline and participate so that you become a working member of the profession. In this way you will learn what others are doing and you will have a balance wheel to counter the niggling problems within your own department that can so easily get out of proportion.

- Respect your own judgment. Of course, you should be aware of the scholarship that has preceded you, but pay close attention to what you see with your own eyes, hear with your own ears, think with your own mind. Ours is not only a profession of confirmation but also of exploration. I have published personal answers to my own questions about how writers read and write, not so much to provide answers as to provoke research, since I have found few people dealing with questions in our discipline which I believe are obvious—and fundamental. If I publish my guesses, others may respond with their truths.

- Write for yourself. Don't try to figure out what other people want but try to figure out what you have to say and how it can be best said. The standards for academic writing are contradictory and confused. In many cases what is considered to be the standard forces bad writing. Most editors want good writing. Decide how best to say what you have to say. You may have to compromise your voice to be published in some journals that require educationese or excessive formality, but certainly do not compromise in advance and write in a parody of academic writing. Submit writing that is as clear and graceful as you can make it.

- Write early. Remember that you are not writing the ultimate article that will cause all other scholars to pack up their tents and go home. Write early to find out what you know and what you need to know. Publish early to participate in the game of academic exploration. You will learn by committing yourself and by developing colleagues in other schools who are interested in the same topics.

• Yet be patient. This is hard for me under any circumstances, for I was born twitching to get on with it, whatever it was. It is often difficult for a young faculty member under the threat of tenure. To be patient, it is important to develop a pace appropriate to the work you are doing. It takes time for ideas to be planted and cultivated. There has to be a habit of work that allows this to happen. Those of us who publish extensively are harvesting what has been put down years before.

Most of my articles have a five-year history. It takes about a year for my reading and thinking and conversing and note making to work their way toward a topic which is more interesting than I had expected. Once I recognize the topic's potential significance I play around with it for at least a year, taking advantage of opportunities to talk on the subject or to teach it. I receive reactions from my colleagues and my students, and then in the third year I may accept a chance to give a paper or to attempt an article. Now I begin to plan in earnest. My play becomes more intense, and eventually there is a paper or a draft. My colleagues, often my students, and my editors or audiences react. In the fourth year it is usually rewritten and edited. And in the fifth year it is published. And to those who do not work continually, it appears as if I had suddenly produced another piece of work, when it is really the product of a rather plodding habit of thinking through writing.

• Write to discover what you have to say. You do not have to know what you want to say to be able to say it. Just the opposite. You have to write to find out what you have to say. This is the never-ending attraction of writing. We write more than we intend to write, reaching beyond our goals, finding within ourselves how much more we know than we thought we knew. We need to write drafts with such speed and intensity that they propel us toward unexpected possibility. Then we can learn from those drafts as we revise and clarify. We are, first of all, students to our own writing.

- Write without notes. Much academic writing is poor because it is note-bound. Write out of what is in your head; write what you remember from your notes. What you forget is probably what should be forgotten, but you will have time after the draft is completed to go back and check your notes. If you absolutely have to have key references in front of you, use as few as possible in producing the first draft in which speed and flow produce both grace and the unexpected connections which are the mark of good thinking and good writing.

- Lower your standards. I carry two paragraphs of counsel from poet and teacher William Stafford with me at all times and turn to them morning after morning:

> I believe that the so-called "writing block" is a product of some kind of disproportion between your standards and your performance. . . . One should lower his standards until there is no felt threshold to go over in writing. It's *easy* to write. You just shouldn't have standards that inhibit you from writing.
>
> I can imagine a person beginning to feel that he's not able to write up to that standard he imagines the world has set for him. But to me that's surrealistic. The only standard I can rationally have is the standard I'm meeting right now. . . . You should be more willing to forgive yourself. It really doesn't make any difference if you are good or bad today. The *assessment* of the product is something that happens *after* you've done it.

- Write easily. If it doesn't come, don't force it. Forced writing reads like forced writing. Putter. Fiddle around. Stare out the window. Keep coming back until your head is ready to produce the writing almost without effort. Hard writing usually means that you're not ready to write. You have to start the writing process early enough ahead of deadline to allow the essential backing up—the planning and rehearsal that will eventually allow the draft to flow. As Virginia Woolf said, "I am going to hold myself from writing it till I have it impending in me: grown heavy in my mind like a ripe pear; pendant, gravid, asking to be cut or it will fall."

- Write with your ear. Writers feel that the voice may be the most important element in writing, and few writers will proceed until they hear the voice of the text. Voice is the magic ingredient in writing. It carries all the meanings that are not within the world. It allows the individual writer to speak to the individual reader. It is style and grace and tone, and it reveals the character of the writer as well as the content of the text.

  Listen for a voice in fragments of writing in your notebook, in lines rehearsed in your head, in early drafts. Your voice will help you understand what you have to say and how you have to say it, and a strong voice will be the element that will make significant content available to your colleagues. It will bring you publication, and publication will bring you the opportunity for further exploration.

- Write writing. Try a poem, a familiar essay that can be published on the editorial page of a newspaper, a novel, a TV or movie script, a magazine article, a short story, a news story, a play. The experience of writing writing, not just writing about writing, will help the soul, the scholarship, and the craft. The poem may not be anthologized, but it may reveal a leap of language, a turn of a line that will free your prose and allow the poet's skills of grace and clarification that are so often missing from academic writing.

- Reach out to colleagues. This will be your most difficult— and the most valuable—professional activity. The academic world can be a closed place, a landscape of monasteries and convents, moated castles and isolated villages. Even when I am intimidated by the walls and parapets erected by colleagues I try to remember how lonely they must be, imprisoned within their knowledge and high standards.

Invite colleagues to lunch, suggest a cup of coffee, ask a colleague to visit your class, set up brown bag lunches of colleagues to share common interests, arrange team teaching, travel together to conventions. Most of all, reach out by sharing your own drafts. I have received insult, scorn, ridicule, jocular remarks that burn like acid, and, worst of all, silence. And for many good reasons. Most of us do not know how to respond, and we are all busy. But through this reaching out in my own department, across my campus, to colleagues I meet at meetings, to students and former students, to friends in other fields, I begin to develop a small group of helpful colleagues in each of the areas in which I work. I share work with them; they share work with me. They know how to give me criticism. But even more important, they know how to give me strength and support. They know because they are writing, are exposed and vulnerable in the same way I am. If we can discover the attitudes and the techniques that allow us to write we will experience the joy of writing. First will come the lonely surprises that occur on the page. A life of writing is a life of learning. There are the tiny discoveries that may not shake the universe but that may bring a grin or sometimes even a laugh of victory from the academic at the desk. Writing is more likely than teaching to produce an active intellectual life and to be a defense against boredom, burnout, and age. The writer can always ask new questions and draft new answers, can always explore new territories and experience new genres.

Writing is also an extension of teaching and a stimulation to teaching. Our students, wave after wave, may change their lingo and their dress, but they remain at the same intellectual level when they come to us. We need to be practitioners of our discipline if we are to stay alive and if we are to bring new ideas to our teaching.

Publishing allows us to belong to a large community of scholars. We can contribute to that community, and the more we put in, the more we will take away that is of value to both ourselves and our students. Publication obviously has its rewards—promotion, tenure, occasional recognition in an elevator at a convention, and even royalties, although most books I have produced have never made their advance. But the more you experience those rewards, the more you realize that the real satisfaction comes during the process of the writing itself. The true rewards are internal—the satisfaction of asking your own questions and finding your own answers.

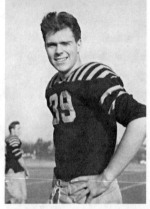

eighteen

Where Was I Headed When I Left?
(1984)

My reading of what writers say about writing is an important form of shop talk for me. It stimulates my thoughts, helps me understand the writing process and often strikes unexpected sparks. A week or so ago I heard Saul Bellow say to me, "With everything I write I draw a little closer to whatever it was that made me wish to be a writer."

I have felt that, too, and a number of other things make me want to consider Bellow's remark:

- My visit to Linda Rief's wonderful 7th grade class. Their writerly questions made me remember again that I was already a writer—for at least three years—when I was in the 7th grade. And I remember the pain and the wonder and the observation and the searching and the loneliness of those years.

- Meeting Isaiah and hearing him say that when the doctor told him that he had five years—or less—because of cancer, that he felt a great sense of freedom. He didn't have to follow the career in which he had not been aware he was following. He re-assessed his life, joined the Peace Corps and found a peace in an African Village that he has been able to maintain since his return. It is five years since the doctor gave him his freedom.

- My sense of passage from 59 to 60. Not a sense of closing down but of opening up. I have not been my father and now I can begin to be whatever it was that I set out to be.

- My impatience with those elements in academic life—and those qualities of academics—with which I should *not* be impatient. It is foolish to be angry at a giraffe for being a giraffe.

- My nostalgia for the loneliness of a strange and sickly childhood when I had time for sitting—just sitting; for reading books in which I could become lost from the world; for conversations with imaginary companions; for a life of fantasy that could allow me to levitate and escape any Sunday afternoon living room—or any Monday afternoon classroom.

- My itch to learn to fly a plane, to study art full time, to do something that I have not done which has the potential for large failure (a tremendous BOOOOOOOM as student pilot hits ridge????) rather than the prediction of a series of tiny, repetitive successes.

- Not so much a fear that I have become the masks that I have learned to wear but a feeling that I can now toss them all to the audience and soft shoe off stage.

Where was I headed anyway and why? What is it that makes a skinny [yes, skinny] kid decide to a writer? Let's get profound. This seminar has been short of profound. What is it that makes someone have the arrogance to think they might be "creative?"

Discomfort

The shoe didn't fit. An egotistical sense of not belonging. Alienation. I am better than this, than these people. An enormous arrogance and sense of self crouching behind an even larger sense of inadequacy. What a great comfort in this self exile. Of course I had an unhappy childhood. I would have made any childhood unhappy. I absolutely refuse to reconsider my carefully manufactured myths. *My* childhood was really pretty average, better than average in fact, no, no, no, they tried to make me eat eggs. Yccckk.

Fantasy

My friends lived in the walls and we talked the day through. They lived in books. They lived in my head. I told myself stories of other times and other places and made the world in which I was living stranger than it was. There were oceans and continents, skies and mountains, planets and rivers and valleys in my head waiting to be explored. Still waiting.

Words

My uncles recited poems to me as they walked the floor with me as a child. My father, the floorwalker, was away taking care of customers and so my uncles walked with me. I heard the great rhymes of the popular poets orated past my ear. My grandmother sang and told stories all day, each with a moral. And the sermons by pastors who could speak in a hundred voices as they acted out the Bible or debated with the Devil and interpreted God. I lived in a house of words. I heard their music, saw that they could make life more than it was, clarify, expand, concentrate, give meaning.

Talent

I was terrified of the story of talents in the Bible. I knew I'd been given something special but I didn't have any idea what it was or what I was to do with it. (Part of my body made me feel the same way.) The more I went to school the worse I did at school. And yet I had talent. It was here somewhere, in this pocket, no, under the bed, in the sugar bowl, somewhere. And I had to do something—what?—with it.

Money

The dream of the movie sale.

173

Love

There are never ever enough ants for the ant eater—or enough applause when they call, "Author! Author!" All the modesty is false but there comes the realization that there will never be enough praise and so, dammit, there must be satisfaction in the doing rather than the done.

Beards

If you look this way, you might as well find a job that fits the figure. Perhaps a Pope waddling forth to the multitudes, smiling, blessing; a bouncer in a Combat zone bar, his back to the girls, the coat open to show the leather strap leading to the bulge under the left armpit; a Professor of English, leaning back against a black board, his hands constructing cathedrals of knowledge, his mouth proclaiming . . . No, that's ridiculous; a dealer, soup on his tie, in a shabby Beacon Hill antique shop who might, in the back room, just happen to . . . A writer! A writer can wear anything, go anywhere, can look like, well, a writer.

Celebration

And we travel back to this. Not for fame or freedom from neckties or love or bucks or escape, not even for understanding or meaning or discovery, perhaps not even for exploration but simply to describe. To see what can't be seen with the eye but may be seen with the word. To catch the memory of the grandmother bending over the crib, her hair still auburn and full, the braid worn like a crown, the light touching each separate strand. To feel again the morning wonder of mud warm and comforting, the earth that rose, then fell with each shell, the kneading of yourself into the ground, the wonder at still being able to reach out an inch, another, and another and feel the cold mud become warm under your hand. To watch again from a sickroom window as the maple leaves moved to follow the sun. To catch it all. What was, what might have been, what was dreamed, imagined, remembered, predicted, connected. To capture what that skinny boy thought wonderful and hold it gently in the double cupped hands and then let it fly away so others will see what I thought at first a bird become a heron. To celebrate.

"That's all? To celebrate? That's it?"
"Yeah."
"What about that novel, the poems, the forms that count?"
"Who's counting?"
"I am."
"Go sit in some marsh grass. Make believe you're Mekeel McBride. Observe the heron."
"My ass'll get wet."
"Yeah."

nineteen

A Writer's Geography

One Writer at Work
(*1991*)

I am going to tell you a story about a story.

This double narrative will tell how I explored an idea that may become an "Over Sixty" column for the *Boston Globe*, a poem, or something I cannot yet imagine while the story itself is being written.

And in taking you into the workshop of the professional writer—he does it for love *and* money—you may see implications for the classroom. In case you don't, I will suggest a few at the end of this experiment.

In the jargon of our age, it is being written in "realtime." I am writing the story of the story while writing the story and there may be no story—but that does not worry me, the sinking of the *Titanic* was far more interesting than the sailing of the *Titanic*. [Remember that if you write with your students.]

And the story of the story cannot be complete. The more I explore my writing processes, the more I am aware of the enormous volume of images, half-memories, quarter thoughts, words, phrases, patterns of words and phrases that pass through my head and are unrecorded. It is a sort of tuning up of the subconscious in preparation for writing.

My conceit is, since we are in Colorado, that I'm an old trail guide, say 67 years of age, and I've been exploring this country since I was a boy. I'm going to take you along on a trip of exploration.

You must understand there is no one way. This is the account of one expedition across the page; each expedition is different, full of surprises, and that is why I haul my creaky bones to the desk and begin.

The real old Colorado guide is familiar with mountains and canyons and rivers; I am familiar with emptiness. I cultivate a receptive awareness to life, free as possible of preconception.

This expedition began last Friday when I drove to the New Hampshire State Prison for Women to work with Kathe Simons in a writing class. I did not intend to write about this experience. I was there as a writer to share my craft and write with the class.

Before and during and after class I tried just to be quiet, to receive, not to sort out, to organize, to focus. I need to remain calm in the middle of the storm of information that was attracted to my memory. I was asked by a student to explain what I meant at one point in the workshop, and I did write some lines about the prisons we all live in on the blackboard, but I did not think I would write about that in a column. But as a writer, I knew there was a bone to worry in what I found myself writing on the board.

After I left the prison, I discovered my random thoughts collecting on a magnet incident. A lovely, dark haired woman—probably nineteen or twenty—told me how much she liked it in prison, that she felt safe there. Later an older inmate said the same thing. I took no quotes, I have no direct quotes but I got the message. Prison was better than what they had come from.

I know I had to—not wanted to, but had to—play with this truth to understand it, or at least to come to terms with it. It was too loud in my brain to be ignored. I thought about it during a lecture I attended in the morning, a football game I went to in the afternoon, during football on TV and a movie on the VCR that night, breakfast and the Sunday papers the next morning.

I must qualify that. "Thought about it" is too formal, too serious a term. My wife, the gardener, says I turn over the compost in my brain. That's more like it. I avoid formal thinking, just toss it to see what is revealed. I make no notes in my daybook, never say to myself in the shower "I'll have to remember that."

At 12:30 on Sunday I go downstairs to my office and my ideal writing environment. Music on the CD player: *The Schutz Musical Exequien*, the meditation on death that influenced Brahms in the construction of his requiem centuries later; football with the sound turned off on TV—the music appropriate to the Patriots facing Pittsburgh.

Normally I write my column Monday morning for the Tuesday a week ahead. I aim for 800 words but can run, on occasion, to 1200. The columns are serious or nostalgic or humorous—sometimes all three—all looking at the world from the point of view of someone over sixty years of age. They usually take about 45 minutes to draft, are edited but rarely revised. If they don't work they are deep-sixed.

I'm starting on Sunday because this story [*Interruption as I edit this Monday. I have 15 minutes to respond to two problems my editor, Evelynne Kramer, sees in tomorrow's column. I pay attention to her! I cut some of the lead. I tried to say two things and I know you can only say one. She thinks I went off on a tangent near the end. I did. Cut that paragraph. She thanks me for delivering it; I thank her for saving me from ridicule. Later, Lauren called from the copy desk. I made up a word. I was proud of the word. She did not think it was an improvement to the language. I trust Lauren and came up with a traditional way of saying it.*] of a story will extend the process many times.

You must understand how little I know at this point in the writing and how little is normally articulated by me to me. Perhaps I can try to catch the fragmented thought in this way: "prison . . . good . . . all in prisons . . . age a prison?" Even that articulation limits my beginning lack of knowledge, my necessary ignorance of what I will say and my openness to what I may say.

I start to write the lead in my head an instant before it will appear on the screen and realize I'm going to start with the inmates' view of prison, but the reader needs the context. I have to set up the prisoner's observation. This is craft and experience, pure and simple.

I think it will be a column, but the idea of a poem keeps coming to mind—or perhaps it is the experience of Colonel Coatse's grandson in the mental ward of a VA hospital who lives in my novel. His prison is a VA psychiatric ward. Maybe it will be all three.

I delay stepping off the diving board into the draft but once I do I know I will finish. Mule-like stubbornness is essential in a writer.

I will start with description and will also have to establish my authority and answer the reader's obvious question why am I at the prison.

> I park on the outside of the high fence and the ~~ominous coils of~~ razor wire coiled at the top of the fence waiting for someone foolish enough to come with its reach. I have come to join a writing class at the New Hampshire State Prison for Women.

I try to use the natural flow of events whenever possible: "I park." I instinctively look for the dominant image: "razor wire." As I write, I cut "ominous coils of" and change the sentence to make the coils of razor wire active, aggressive, then say simply why I am there.

It is very important for me to write fast—dumbly—to outrun the censor and cause the accidents of insight and language necessary for an effective piece of writing. This story of a story is slowing me down. It is a major abnormality in the telling of this double narrative, but then my Colorado trail guide would move fast alone then travel slowly when he guides a bunch of tourists into the wilderness. We'll see how it works.

> I leave my wallet, my key chain with its pocket knife, locked in the car as instructed and take only my car key and my license with me. They are turned in after I sign in.

I cheated. I used spellcheck to get license right. I also said I did what I should have done. Actually I took the knife in and then sent it back out but that was complicated and added nothing to the story.

In that paragraph I wrote simple narrative description that isn't really so simple to do. In a sense I feel that my whole life of craft has been dedicated to learning how to write those two simple sentences. I am reminded of what Hokusai, the great Japanese artist said, "I have drawn things since I was six. All that I made before the age of sixty-five is not worth counting. At seventy-three I began to understand the true construction of animals, plants, trees, birds, fishes, and insects. At ninety I will enter into the secret of things. At a hundred and ten, everything—every dot, every dash—will live." I am 67 and still learning to be simple.

To know where I need to go next I do not look to rhetorical tradition, past experience, rule books, I look at the paragraph I have just written. What comes next? I am in the prison. What's it like? What are the prisoners like?

> I pass through double locked doors, smell the institutional food, learn the institutional meal schedule [breakfast at 6:30, lunch at 10:30, dinner at 3:30], feel the constant vigilance of the guards, see the coiled razor wire through the narrow windows and realize the prisoners look as ordinary as women in the supermarket aisles, perhaps younger on average, more attractive, less frightening than a housewife ~~with a relative coming to dinner~~ heading for a bargain roast.

I am aware of the long sentence—very long for a newspaper—but I use the long paragraph because I want to move the reader through a number of impressions. I also want to reveal with specifics—show, don't tell—and allow the reader to experience the surprise of their ordinariness. I cut my excess: "with a relative coming to dinner." I have to write such lines to see if they work and then cut them if they don't.

Two o'clock, time to carry in some baskets of pears for Minnie Mae, to stretch, to snack. I know where I will be headed when I return—the women in the prison aren't ordinary.

Rain. No pears but lunch, football—the requiem was appropriate—a nap on the chair, a walk in the rain, a trip to return some video tapes, and back to the office to write the 300 new words that is my daily discipline on the novel. The column, of course, has been floating around in the back of my brain, tumbling like a space walker so I can see it in different ways and hear it in different lines as they drift by. Some I watch, some I listen to, but I make no notes, if those images, those lines are passing by now, they will pass by later.

I actually got 350 new words on the novel, interrupted by a long call from a daughter home from her honeymoon, the Buffalo football game on all the time.

Now it is 6:34, I am upstairs, the football game is on, Sunday night supper will be late. I put the lap desk across my chair, fire up the laptop computer and start writing.

> But these are not ordinary women. They have been convicted of theft, prostitution, crimes against person and property, in a few cases they have committed murder, in most cases their crimes have been drug related.

I want to be direct, specific but not judgmental. The reader asks so why should we care about these women? A draft is always a conversation with the reader. The writer must hear the reader and answer the reader's questions.

> They have all had victims, but they are also victims. Most of them have been mistreated by the men in their lives—grandfathers, fathers, uncles, brothers, husbands, lovers. Most are mothers, and good mothers or not they are separated from their children.

That paragraph breeds another. I heard myself say "bright but uneducated" when I described my prison visit to my daughter on the phone. Now I pluck it out of the air and use it.

> The women are bright but uneducated. Their writing demonstrates their talent; their speech reveals they come from the under class. They have not done well in school and have had no help at home. But the talent shines through in their poems and stories, and their intelligence shines through in their questions and their conversation.

I get impatient at this point in the draft to rush to the point of surprise for me—and the reader: the point at which I hope the essay will deepen and reveal the significance of all I have written. I need to write my way toward that, and I remind myself that I can always cut.

> From what I can see the prison has an excellent education program, but it is a prison. Out the window I see the razor wire, inside the class some of the students rock *back and forth, back and forth, others get up and move around, talk to each other; and everyone is controlled* ~~demonstrate other evidence of tension, and the class is interrupted~~ by commands from a speaker that plucks ~~people~~ the inmates out of class and dumps them back in an uneven tidal flow. ~~The institution controls their lives.~~

It's fun to rework a paragraph like this. If I say they are tense, I must show it. I have no choice. If I can use the verb *controlled,* I can cut out the last sentence. *People* is general; *inmates* is specific—and describes what they are and how they are treated. Now I am at the point that sparked the piece.

> I have sympathy for their incarceration but when I talk to a ~~beautiful~~ *dark haired* young woman perhaps nineteen or twenty, ~~with dark hair and eyes~~, she says that she is glad to be here, it is the safest place she has ever been. Later, an older woman says the same thing, and I realize something of the world from which they have come—and to which they will return.

Now I have come to the point where something has to happen. I think I may find something to say about prisons but I do not know what it will be—and if it will turn out to be worth saying. I have to have faith: something usually happens, but the ice is thin and black and bending to the weight of the so-far-written text.

And it is time to eat supper. I save and backup on the computer. Food before art any time.

Now it is Monday morning—Happy Birthday to me—and I scan the last few paragraphs of the column and draft another paragraph born of the last paragraph. It doesn't come instantly and I make myself sit quietly, waiting, receptive, allowing my thoughts to circle and then, I hope, come together in a line or phrase.

> I had not thought of a prison as a haven but after I have contemplated a life in which a young woman finds safety, comfort and quiet in prison, I find myself reflecting on the prisons in which we place ourselves.

I have arrived at the turning point. Usually this moment is a surprise but today I am not totally surprised. It echoes back to what I wrote on the blackboard in that classroom, but it is a turn of thought, a step that is necessary if the column is to be an essay. I am not reporting on women's prisons or on women in prison but thinking about prisons. I must put the experience into a personal, meaningful context, give it a meaning that will not give the reader my thinking but cause the reader to think for herself and himself.

I am aware of a passing instinct as I start to write: I will end on the prison of age. That will come at the point of emphasis in the paragraph—the end—and it may give me a launching pad for the run of thought that will take me to the end of the column. And, suddenly, I have a vision of the end: that young woman will have to have courage to leave prison and we will need courage to leave our prisons of age. I may also mention the hospital experience of mine I shared with her. I realize I never would write this all down if it were not for this talk. I would keep it loose, purposely vague until the moment of drafting.

[I am called to the bathroom. That is worth mentioning because when I did a protocol study with Dr. Carol Berkenkotter they found blanks on the tapes. When I returned I always had solved a writing problem. They found out where I was and called them bathroom epiphanies.]

> Many of us incarcerate ourselves in prisons of our choice—prisons of neighborhood, of class, or religion, of ethnic origin, of sex, of vocation, of prejudice, of age.

It is hard for me to stop and comment. Normally I would be writing fast, paying no attention to syntax, diction, sentence structure,

rhetorical tradition, mechanics, usage, spelling, certainly not spelling, as I try to contain the flood of thought that is pouring from
brain to finger.

In school we teach logical thinking and I am anal compulsive,
love charts, delight in the movement from A to B to C, from
Roman numeral I to Roman numeral II, but while writing I usually
practice associative thinking, swinging like an orangutan from one
handy vine to another, allowing chance to lead me to meaning.
Perhaps we should teach this ape-thinking in school.

> Especially age. This morning I have a birthday. I am yet
> another year over sixty and glad to be here. I do not
> understand the fear some of my peers have of birth-
> days. At this time in my life, I am always glad to have
> another one.

I am focusing the column on one kind of prison and introduc-
ing a mild touch of humor to give the reader some relief and a little
room. It also allows the reader to identify with the writing.

> But my first birthday thoughts are not all cheery. The
> morning Globe seems full of death and deceit, and that
> is topped by the TV news. I am momentarily disturbed
> by our ever changing world that seems to have acceler-
> ated—or is it that I have slowed down? Our home
> seems full of projects to do that may never be done. I
> wonder if the time will come to sell and move into a
> smaller place, perhaps a retirement community.

I am writing dumbly, the way a writer ought to write, allowing
the language of the written text to think. I am not writing what I
have thought, but writing catches me in the act of thinking—if you
are lucky.

> And my thoughts return to that young woman and her
> need for prison. Many of us elderlies come to a time
> when we cannot care for ourselves, when we need the
> structure and protection of a community. We know that
> time may come for us, and this month we pay our nurs-

ing home insurance premium, but I fear the intellectual walls that so many of my peers need when they move into a community of PLU's— [People Like Us]. In one day in Florida I was in a community where that phrase was a code word for anti-semitism and in the same afternoon in another, where it was a code for anti-goyism.

A bit long. May have to be cut. I like the twist of language in "us elderlies," a turn of phrase that is purposefully awkward and incorrect. In my argument I need to recognize that many over-sixties, ourselves included, may have to join a retirement "prison."

As we grow old, our fears of difference often grow stronger. We fear for the safety of our increasingly frail bodies and we fear for the comfort of our minds [?]. I feel the temptation myself when I think I may be forced off the sidewalk by some young punks or forced off the familiar path of thought by a shocking new idea, sound or picture. It would be easy to flee to the prison of age; there is plenty of excuse for retreat.

Again, I do not want to lecture others but to focus on myself, so the reader who would resist a sermon might allow himself or herself to consider my case.

I have friends who are in their sixties and seventies, but outside of my best friend, Minnie Mae, only one close friend is over sixty, others are in their fifties, forties, thirties; they are male and female, black and white, Jewish and Christian, heterosexual and lesbian, some even vote for Republicans. I creak when I walk but feel 18 in my view of the world because of the differences I welcome into my life.

I love lists, litanies, that lead me to places I do not expect to go.

I was honored when I was invited out of my prison and into the women's prison. These women, so mistreated by men, welcomed me into their community, shared their worlds with me, taught me the comfort of prisons, yet made me understand the need for leaving prison.

I'm really pushing to get to the end and will rethink the logic of what I am saying later. Now a paragraph that may be a bit too much but will speak to many of my readers.

> I was eager to leave the prison of the hospital after my by-pass but when we stopped at a large drug store on the way home and I found myself alone in an aisle, out of sight of my wife and daughter, I felt a dreadful fear of freedom. I won that lonely battle, but I realize that it is not easy to leave hospitals or other prisons.

Now I'll see if the ending I had a hint of paragraphs ago will work.

> I do not face the terrors that young woman will face when she leaves prison, but we will have some of the same apprehensions of difference and choice. I hope we, young and old, fortunate and unfortunate, will find a way to escape prison, pass through our fears, and celebrate the ever changing, ever frightening, ever new world in which we live.

Too Pollyannish? I have to stand back from the essay. I had to make the commitment. I can change, qualify, kill the draft. I will read it over and edit it; have Minnie Mae read it; Kathe Simons, the teacher of the writing class, read it; and send it to Evelynne Kramer, my editor at the *Boston Globe,* who will read it. But first I have to read it through myself, with detachment, line by line.

First I need to run a spellcheck—several words a paragraph are misspelled *after* I had checked the spelling once myself—and get a word count: 1094, a bit long but no major problem. Now I will read it through carefully, for thought and voice, pace and proportion, specificity and reader understanding.

I make changes in language in my reading, making the draft more specific, more direct, more graceful. I make little changes of style. I pay attention to Chekhov who taught me that "If in the first chapter you say that a gun hung on the wall, in the second or third chapter it must without fail be discharged." I document each point that needs documentation.

But I need other readers to reassure me I have written something worth publishing, that I have made sense, that I am writing with both clarity and grace. I need readers who hear my voice and help me make it stronger; who are constructive not destructive; candid and specific.

Minnie Mae tells me it is worth publishing, changes the punctuation that does seem, as always, to clarify the meaning and questions the spots that need questioning.

Kathe Simons had never read a piece of mine in draft before. I will ask her to read others in the future. She knew how to tell me what worked and to spot the places I knew needed work once she had pointed them out. I clarified and cut lines in the lead, and she was the one who gave me the idea of identity that I carried a bit further than she meant in the second paragraph. I read her comments and made the article much better.

A good reader is a treasure every writer needs. They are rare and I exploit every good reader I find.

I get a message on the answering machine that my editor, Evelynne Kramer, thinks that the piece needs more work—but she has gone home. I throw a temper tantrum—age four, Richter Scale 9.7—because I didn't get the message in time to talk to her, but get up the next morning and quickly write the following column in case it is deep sixed and I leave for Colorado.

> The toy I remember best from my childhood was an empty Quaker Oats box. I hated porridge—one of the benefits of being over sixty is that I never, ever will have to eat globs of hot cereal again—but I loved my drum, my castle tower, my tunnel, my wheel, my echo box, my cave, my hat.
>
> I was reminded of that wonderful toy, because as a new grandfather I have discovered the warehouse toy store with shelves up to the roof stacked with toys that

require grandparental credit cards, but often require little imagination on the part of a child.

I will add to the gross national product and buy toys that demonstrate that I am a grandfather in good working order, but I will also make sure that Joshua has a large, round, Quaker Oats box.

What toys await him in his expanding world! I am not a great fan of oriental rugs, but I believe I could trace—right now—the pattern of our living room rug in the house on Grand View Avenue. I remember its deep red, its bright but fading blue. My fingers traveled its maze of roads a thousand times.

It was probably on that rug that I first discovered shadows, my afternoon companions, and later, reflections that darted up walls and cavorted on the ceiling.

Perhaps it was a reflection that introduced me to the family that lived in the wall. An only child, I lived a secret life with a family of small people, rich with brothers and sisters with whom I could always talk. Entering the wall, I could live and travel far beyond the house. And they ate no porridge! I wish Joshua such wonderful companions.

I can remember a glass doored bookcase in which I first was aware that the tadpole figure with its bobbing head was me. If I moved, it moved. I've recently been caught doing a hop, skip, and jump in front of a store window in a mall. Surprise, the fat man with the white beard in the glass performed the same dancing steps.

The other day Joshua rolled over on his back for the first time and howled. His world had turned upside down, perhaps he was on the ceiling looking down.

I would like to be with him when he climbs his first tree. Of course, I would probably spoil it and order him down, "right this minute" or hover under him, a safety net that would rob him of private adventure.

I was never so high when I stepped out of a plane in the paratroops as I was on the first, second, and sometimes even third branch of an apple tree in the back yard on Vassell Street. Years later I revisited that tree. It was tiny, really a sturdy bush, but I could remember my discovery of height.

I was in the world of birds. I was safe from the airedale looking up, and laughed at his barking, his terrible tongue, his wolf teeth. I could even see across the fence into the Coughlin's yard and peer into our dining room window spying on Grandma setting the table for supper.

Already I am looking at jungle gyms to buy for Joshua, now three months old. They have swings and slides and rope climbs and ladders and tree houses with canvas roofs. I may buy him one, but it will never take the place of a tree.

My first airplane rides, when I flew Grandma back to Scotland for the afternoon, were constructed with two living room wicker chairs, tipped over, and a piano stool on its side. It will be necessary for Joshua to have a piano stool that twirls. No piano bench can take its place.

As I relive my childhood to discover the world in which Joshua will adventure, I remember my caves: under the dining room table, under the basement stairs, behind the living room couch. And outside, the secret, dark, dank, terrifying and wonderful under porch where the spiders drew me pictures on air.

If we give Joshua no toys, he will have childhood. He will climb the wooden mountain of the stairs, explore the caverns and mines of underbed, play the spoon orchestra.

And if he is lucky he will never lose the wonder of life. I admit I feared second childhood. I was wrong.

My walls are still filled with invisible friends that walk the pages of my novel. Early in the morning I beat out a dance with spoon on jelly jar, mug, and plate. Flying at 36,000 feet I track the jungle animals in the clouds far below.

I do not intend to teach my grandson to play but to take instruction from him, rediscover the texture—and taste—of grass, become astonished at the amazing way a ball can leave one person's hand and arrive in another's, learn again how satisfying it is to hear the story when you know the end.

This is the professional at work. One piece may not work, write another. As E. L. Doctorow says, "The writing generates the writing." Before my editor gets to work, an alternate column is on her desk.

At ten AM I call Evelynne who feels the prison column gets off track when I mention my birthday, that I struggle with the parallel between prisons. I need to sharpen, to clarify my thoughts; I need to make the voluntary prison idea clearer. The ending isn't tight enough.

I respect her judgment and feel she's probably right. I wanted her to read it early because I felt it was forced—it was—and I am eager to get at it again. As Neil Simon says, "In baseball you only get three swings and you're out. In rewriting, you get almost as many swings as you want and you know, sooner or later, you'll hit the ball." I don't see rewriting as failure but opportunity.

And my dialogue with my editor is interesting. She has to be supportive enough so I will write, critical enough so that I will rewrite; specific enough to at least circle the problem, vague enough to allow me to make my own discoveries. For me, Evelynne is the ideal editor.

Now I read the draft, scalpel held casually at the ready. I agree with Evelynne but do not see the solution. I will cut the piece in half and toss the second half away. I number the paragraphs, something I've never done. It will keep me busy while my subconscious works.

1. I park on the outside of the high fence where the razor wire coiled at the top of the fence waits for someone foolish enough to come within its reach. I have come to join a writing class at the New Hampshire State Prison for Women.

2. I leave my wallet, my key chain with its pocket knife, locked in the car as instructed, and take only my car key and my license with me. I sign in and they take my key and my identity.

3. I pass through double locked doors, smell the institutional food, learn the institutional meal schedule [breakfast at 6:30, lunch at 10:30, dinner at 3:30], feel the constant vigilance of the guards, see the coiled razor wire through the narrow windows and realize the prisoners look as ordinary as women in the supermarket aisles, perhaps younger on average, more attractive, less frightening than a housewife heading for bargain chicken quarters.

4. But these are not ordinary women. They have been convicted of theft, prostitution, crimes against person and property; in a few cases they have committed murder, in most cases their crimes have been drug related.

5. They have all had victims, but they are also victims. Many have been mistreated by their mothers but most of them have been mistreated by the men in their lives—grandfathers, fathers, uncles, brothers, husbands, lovers. Most are mothers and traditional mothers or not they are separated from their children.

6. The women are bright but uneducated. Their writing demonstrates their talent; their speech reveals most come from the under class, the class most of us try to make invisible. They have not done well in school and have had little help at home or from society. But the talent shines through in their poems and stories, and their intelligence shines through in their questions and their conversations.

7. From what I saw in a brief visit the prison has an education program with dedicated teachers, but the classroom is in a prison. Out the window I see the razor wire; inside the class some of the students rock back and forth, back and forth; others get up and move around, talk to each other; and everyone is controlled by commands from a speaker that plucks the inmates out of class and dumps them back in an uneven tidal flow.

8. I have sympathy for their incarceration, but when I talk to a lovely young woman perhaps nineteen or twenty, with dark hair and eyes, she says that she is glad to be here, it is the safest place she has ever been. Later, an older woman says the same thing, and I try to imagine the worse-than-prison world from which they have come—and to which they will return.

> I will keep the first eight paragraphs. Should I stay with those women, go deeper inside myself [the prison of compulsive work] or try to make clearer the blurred statement I made in the last draft that I am not sure I understand?

~~9. I had not thought of a prison as a haven but after I contemplated a life in which a young woman finds safety, comfort and quiet in prison, I find myself reflecting on the prisons in which we all place ourselves.~~

~~10. Many of us incarcerate ourselves in prisons of our choice—prisons of neighborhood, of class, or religion, of ethnic origin, of sex, of vocation, of prejudice, of age.~~

I might save paragraphs 9 and 10. Might. I will deep six the last eight. Right now. Delete! Now I have six or eight paragraphs of brilliance to produce. Panic. Calm. I will be calm. OOOOOOOOOM. I read back like a person trying to leap from one apartment roof to another, hoping I will develop the momentum to carry me to the other side. I skip paragraphs 9 and 10 and take off from try to imagine.

9. I cannot. But with frightening clarity I once more experience a familiar scene from my childhood, my mother striding back and forth in our railroad flat, chanting, "If I had the wings of an angel, over these prison walls would I fly."

10. She felt imprisoned in her marriage, by caring for her invalid mother, by trying to understand her teenage son, by trying to deny her true feelings and live the life her society and her religion told her she should live.

11. My grandmother, who had been an enormously powerful woman, was imprisoned in bed by a "shock." My father who wanted to be a minister or a teacher—and should have been—was imprisoned in retailing by an eighth grade education.

12. And these women in the classroom all have similar prisons plus the one with razor wire fences and unexpected body searches. My folks, unhappy as they were, were lucky by the standards of the women in this room, but what I took from the prison was not only a feeling of good fortune for the way my life has turned out but of wonder at the strength of the human spirit.

13. In that room I found humor, honesty, little self pity, a great deal of caring for each other, and a powerful determination to survive.

14. I recognize the realities of that room: tests that read HIV positive, marriage to husbands in the men's prison, acts that can never be undone, failure to survive outside again and again and again, the repeated seduction of suicide, brains with the connecting wires melted by drugs, children who are in foster homes or worse; yet from the sadness, the pain, the individual loneliness, I heard voices in poems and stories that inspire.

15. Not many will make it, but some will and they, not the children of privilege, will be the ones to teach us the meaning and value of our lives. I went to teach and, as so often happens, I learned.

Eight hundred and four words—less is more again. Mozart's double piano concertos for two and three pianos helped, but what is important is that I went back through the text that worked into the experience in the classroom itself, not thinking about what I saw but reliving that time in the classroom, re-seeing the faces, rehearing the voices, once more shaking their hands.

I read it through, sharpening, shaping, doubting the text and, because of the deadline, put my doubts aside. I send it in and go off to lunch and a meeting. If another draft is needed, I will try it in late afternoon.

I called Evelynne and she said, "That's better," end of conversation. It will run—after a careful reading by the copy desk. I'll hear from a copy editor next Monday.

In closing I would like to go back over this expedition and point out some things I see that may have implications for the classroom. I expect you will see others—and not agree with all of mine. Good. My theology is based on difference.

Some of the implications for the classroom may be:
* Emphasize awareness—the revealing specific, the direct quote, the action taken and the action not taken, the instigating fact, the loading of the conscious, the subconscious, even the unconscious.

- Allow time for mulling over, for thoughtful delay.
- Respect students' associative, subconscious ape-thinking as they swing from the vine of one thought to another.
- Teach students to pay attention to—and respect—their own thoughts and feelings by respecting them yourself.
- Help students develop the courage to write—and read— what they did not expect to write.
- Welcome stubbornness, the determination to finish, the suspension of critical judgment until there is a draft.
- Preach the importance of description and narration, not usually respected by college—and some high powered high school—English departments.
- Demonstrate the importance of looking within the text for the trail towards meaning and the solution to writing problems.
- Demand students answer the questions the reader will most certainly ask.
- Discuss the possibility of weaving writing into their life.
- Show in your response to their drafts the need for good readers of work in process. Help them become readers as well as writers of their own drafts and their classmates' drafts.

I hope this expedition has not been mysterious but rather ordinary, almost boring. That you will say, "What was that all about? I do that—and my students can do that."

Good. Go do it.

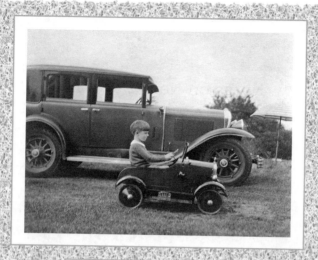

twenty

Notes on Narrative Time
(2001)

- In life and in narrative, we know that a clock is ticking, that time is moving forward, that every event is marked by time: the present is becoming the past as the future is becoming the present. The reader knows this and is discomforted and confused when the narrative goes against what I call natural time. Readers will not recognize the problem, they will just stop reading.

- We can go back in memory with a draft, but it is memory with its own clock that is ticking and moving forward. The memory must move forward on its own time parallel to the clock of the main narrative.

- Do not start at the beginning, but at a moment of intensity. Readers must be engaged, then they will want the information the writer has to deliver. In the revision of the memoir I have just delivered, *The Lively Shadow—Living with a Child Who Left Before You*, I begin at the moment of removing extraordinary means and letting her go, then go back to Lee's conception and life, then her sickness and our waiting for the crisis to pass, her gift of death [described in the beginning] and the 24 years since.

- It is a good general rule to start as near the end as possible. This compresses time, allows the reader to explore deeply and makes it possible for the writer to deliver background information within the moment, when the reader wants and needs it.

- As much as possible our stories should move forward in natural time. I consciously worked on this for years. Running against natural time or a natural sequence is a major problem in organization. Readers' problems—or discomforts—may simply be that information is not being delivered in the order it would be experienced in life.

- A fine woman magazine writer nearly 50 years ago in the pre-computer age when I did at least three drafts, reading each at least ten times [Yes, thirty readings] suggested I literally cut one draft into separate paragraphs, spread out those individual paragraphs on floor, bed or table and move them around until I found the natural order. I did that for years to solve problems of logic, sequence, and time or chronology.

- If I have to write a transition or use a transitional phrase— "meanwhile back at the ranch," "in retrospect," "previously," and so forth I have failed to find the natural order in which the information should have been delivered to the reader. Transitions are a sign you have not gotten the order right. In editing, I try to move the information where it belongs—where readers know they need it. I try never to write formal transitions.

  - *Side note. When I became Freshman English Director I discovered that some staff members were handing out lists of transitional phrases, requiring their students to use them since they believed frequent transitional phrases were a mark of formal academic writing and a busy intellect.*

- We also know that although the clock ticks evenly like a metronome that life is experienced unevenly. The 47 seconds when my chute didn't open and I had to release and feed out my reserve chute that then tangled with another jumper so that I had to retrieve my knife from my leg scabbard and cut myself free from the other jumper and then land is not equal to 47 seconds when I was waiting to jump. [*Long sentence used purposefully to dramatize much of what I had to do in 47 second jump.*]

- Beginning writers must learn to expand the moment and get through the time between moments as quickly as possible. A helpful image may be a necklace [a rosary?] with large and small beads strung on string of time. The more time we cover, usually means less depth; the more we compress time, the deeper we can go into experience.

- The moment—compressed time—should usually be more limited than the beginning writer can imagine. Within the 47 seconds I had time to calmly perform a series of acts. In writing about it I can slow and expand the moment so I could explore the social climate of World War II, move back and explore my childhood, examine why it was necessary for me to volunteer for the paratroops at 18, project into the future examining how this training helped me during combat or, later, during the dying of the child.

- The moment is a bubble of time that has its own past, present, and future, but the writer should move within this bubble of time in as natural an order as possible.

- We must be aware of how much time readers need to comprehend—experience and understand—an event. The pace of time is vital. If we give readers too much time they lose interest and stop reading; too little time and they become confused and stop reading. We must allow the reader time to absorb the experience and respond to it emotionally and intellectually.

- It is a waste of time to give background first, begin the narrative later. Readers will not hold out of time the information the writer knows they will need later but that readers do *not* know they will need.

- We must engage in a conversation with the reader and *listen* to the reader. The reader will need information, saying

"What was that?" "How come?" "What's this going to mean?" "Where did this start?" and other profound questions such as "Huh?" and "No shit?" If we answer those questions when they are asked no transitions or flashback or flash forwards are needed. Information delivered when the reader wants or needs it or, ideally both, does not mean a movement back in time The information is being delivered in the moment, the natural time of the narrative.

- The excellent writer anticipates the reader's need for information. Timing is everything. A great player delivers the puck or basketball where the receivers will be in evolving time. They get the puck or ball when they need it—many times not knowing they are at the place and at the moment they need it to score. The writer learns to deliver past and even future information at the place the reader needs it. No time marker is necessary. Information arrives as needed, timed to the chronology of experience or thought within the reader's brain.

- All writing, poetry, fiction, drama and all the varieties of nonfiction—personal essay and impersonal essay, argument, description and exposition, research report, scholarly journal article, business memo, CIA account, proposal, biography and autobiography, textbook, thesis, and dissertation—are all narrative. The reader moves forward according to an emotional or intellectual chronology or both. We are all storytellers.

twenty-one

Two Poems

BACK ROW, SIXTH GRADE
It is always October.
I trudge to school,
kick a stone, leap the crack
that goes to China,
take my seat in the back row, jam
my knees under the desk,
avoiding chewing gum, waiting
for recess. The substitute
teacher hesitates
by the door. The bell
rings. She commands
attention to the text.
I cannot find my place.
There is no meaning
in the words. Nearsighted,
I squint at the blackboard:
the tails of dogs, a banana,
a winding river, a diving
hawk. I am in the wrong grade,
in a foreign school, another
century. I stare out the window,
learn how a robin drives a squirrel
from her nest, imagine
a fear of wings. Teacher
calls my name. I speak,
as surprised as if a bee
flew from my mouth.

Don dedicated some of his books to his wife, Minnie Mae, "who shares my words and my life" and "who made soup out of old bones and mailed out manuscripts in which I had no faith."

MINNIE MAE COOKS A POEM
She decides to make lentil soup
but there are no lentils,

remembers soup begins with what you have at hand,
what is left over, ripe or not yet quite
rotten, what demands to be saved.

She examines the bones saved against
need: a turkey carcass, one pork chop
with no pork, shin bone that was intended
for the neighbor's dog but kept, steak bones,
pig's knuckles, chicken wings, lamb leg,
selects the ones that have not cooked
together before, imagines their soup.

When they fill the pot, she adds water,
turns up the flame.

In the evening she skims off the fat,
smells in the steam what she does not
expect: meals and friends, the house after
they leave, family worries, celebrations and, yes,
sees hunt, capture, the butcher cleaver
coming down.

Still she must make soup, there is a need
for what is not wasted.

The next day, she reaches under the counter,
chooses six red potatoes, 10 yellow onions,
cuts them in quarters, scrapes one bunch

of carrots, slices, hacks a turnip
into squares, then beets.

Root crops were her ancestors' winter food.

She skims off more fat, adds what is cut and cleaned,
puts the cover back on.

From refrigerator she takes a half head of cabbage,
the celery not yet eaten, last night's limas,
Sunday's peas, some of the fresh broccoli
bought for tomorrow's dinner, and yes,
the cauliflower that was not dipped
when those people who knew her
in another life dropped by
unannounced.

Stir and taste.
It is not what she expects.
She smiles and fits the cover tight.

Friday's summer squash smells all right,
dump it in. Slice last week's sausage, Italian hot,
three picnic hot dogs, one with mustard, trim the tomatoes
that need saving, and the peppers red and green and yellow
turning brown. Cut away what is too far gone,
preserve what is left.

She adds, stirs, notes how this steaming spoonful
tastes so different from the last. It is at last
making itself soup. She turns down the light,
lets it simmer until she goes to bed.

In the morning she wakes to the dream
of grandma's soup, thick as stew.

From the freezer, she selects last summer's
shishkabob, a cup of venison stew, one and one half
hamburg patties. Surprise. There is lentil soup.
She puts in the pot with shells and angel hair, marinara
and white clam sauce, these frozen salad greens will fit
right in. And oh, yes, where is that bag of spinach? Good, I
can save half the leaves. Stir them in.

She shakes in salt, grinds in pepper, dribbles in a touch of soy,
stirs and sips, adds some more and a dash of Worcestershire,
another shake, a third. It will make a company meal.

She forgets the garlic, hurries to peel one toe,
two, three.

She adds the rice left over from the Chinese chicken and
    cashews
ordered in, finds the chicken and cashews, plops
them in as well, and stirs,
then tastes.

It is not what she has ever cooked before.

Minnie Mae serves it steaming in their bowls,
watches as they taste, find the flavors
they need to make her soup their own.

twenty-two

All Writing Is Autobiography
(1991)

I publish in many forms—poetry, fiction, academic article, essay, newspaper column, newsletter, textbook, juvenile nonfiction and I have even been a ghost writer for corporate and government leaders—yet when I am at my writing desk I am the same person. As I look back, I suspect that no matter how I tuned the lyre, I played the same tune. All my writing—and yours—is autobiographical.

To explore this possibility, I want to share a poem that appeared in the March 1990 issue of *Poetry*.

> AT 64, TALKING WITHOUT WORDS
> The present comes clear when rubbed
> with memory. I relive a childhood
> of texture: oatmeal, the afternoon rug,
> spears of lawn, winter finger tracing
> frost on window glass, August nose
> squenched against window screen. My history
> of smell: bicycle oil, leather catcher's
> mitt, the sweet sickening perfume of soldiers
> long dead, ink fresh on the first edition.
> Now I am most alone with others, companioned
> by silence and the long road at my back,
> mirrored by daughters. I mount the evening

stairs with mother's heavy, wearied
step, sigh my father's long complaint.
My beard grows to the sepia photograph
of a grandfather I never knew. I forget
if I turned at the bridge, but arrive
where I intended. My wife and I talk
without the bother of words. We know Lee
is 32 today. She did not stay twenty
but stands at each room's doorway. I place
my hand on the telephone. It rings.

What is autobiographical in this poem? I was 64 when I wrote
it. The childhood memories were real once I remembered them by
writing. I realized I was mirrored by daughters when the line
arrived on the page. My other daughter would have been 32 on
the day the poem was written. Haven't you all had the experience
of reaching for the phone and hearing it ring?

There may even be the question of autobiographical language.
We talk about our own language, allowing our students their own
language. In going over this draft my spellcheck hiccupped at
squenched and *companioned*. As an academic I gulped; as a writer
I said, "Well, they are now."

Then Brock Dethier, one of the most perceptive of the test
readers with whom I share drafts, pointed out the obvious—where
all the most significant information is often hidden. He answered
my question, "What is autobiographical in this poem?" by saying,
"Your thinking style, your voice." Of course.

We are autobiographical in the way we write; my autobiography exists in the examples of writing I use in this piece and in the
text I weave around them. I have my own peculiar way of looking
at the world and my own way of using language to communicate
what I see. My voice is the product of Scottish genes and a Yankee
environment, of Baptist sermons and the newspaper city room, of
all the language I have heard and spoken.

In writing this paper I have begun to understand, better than I
ever have before, that all writing, in many different ways, is auto-

biographical, and that our autobiography grows from a few deep taproots that are set down into our past in childhood.

Willa Cather declared, "Most of the basic material a writer works with is acquired before the age of fifteen." Graham Greene gave the writer five more years, no more: "For writers it is always said that the first 20 years of life contain the whole of experience—the rest is observation."

Those of us who write have only a few topics. My poems, the novel I'm writing, and some of my newspaper columns keep returning to my family and my childhood, where I seek understanding and hope for a compassion that has not yet arrived. John Hawkes has said, "Fiction is an act of revenge." I hope not, but I can not yet deny the importance of that element in my writing. Revenge against family, revenge against the Army and war, revenge against school.

Another topic I return to is death and illness, religion and war, a great tangle of themes. During my childhood I began the day by going to see if my grandmother had made it through the night; I ended my day with, "Now I lay me down to sleep, I pray the Lord my soul to keep. If I should die before I wake, I pray the Lord my soul to take."

I learned to sing "Onward Christian Soldiers Marching as to War," and still remember my first dead German soldier and my shock as I read that his belt buckle proclaimed God was on *his* side. My pages reveal my obsession with war, with the death of our daughter, with that territory I explored in the hours between the bypass operation that did not work and the one that did.

Recently, Boynton/Cook–Heinemann published *Shoptalk*, a book I began in Junior High School that documents my almost lifelong fascination with how writing is made. I assume that many people in this audience are aware of my obsession with writing and my concern with teaching that began with my early discomfort in school that led to my dropping out and flunking out. My academic writing is clearly autobiographical.

Let's look now at a Freshman English sort of personal essay, what I like to call a reflective narrative. I consider such pieces of writing essays, but I suppose others think of them in a less inflated way as newspaper columns. I write a column, *Over Sixty,* for the *Boston Globe,* and the following one was published October 10th of 1989. It was based on an experience I had the previous August.

Over sixty brings new freedoms, a deeper appreciation of life and the time to celebrate it, but it also brings, with increasing frequency, such terrible responsibilities as sitting with the dying.

Recently it was my turn to sit with my brother-in-law as he slowly left us, the victim of a consuming cancer.

When I was a little boy, I wanted—hungered—to be a grown-up. Well, now I am a grown-up. And when someone had to sit with the dying on a recent Saturday, I could not look over my shoulder. I was the one. My oldest daughter will take her turn. She is a grown-up as well, but those of us over sixty have our quota of grown-upness increase. Time and again we have to confront crisis: accident, sickness, death. There is no one else to turn to. It is our lonely duty.

Obligation has tested and tempered us. No one always measures up all the time. We each do what we can do, what we must do. We learn not to judge if we are wise, for our judgments boomerang. They return. At top speed and on target.

Most of us, sadly and necessarily, have learned to pace ourselves. We have seen friends and relatives destroyed by obligation, who have lost themselves in serving others. There is no end to duty for those who accept it.

And we have seen others who diminish by shirking responsibility. When we call them for help the door is shut. We hear silence.

We grow through the responsible acceptance of duty, obligation balanced by self-protection. We teeter along a high wire trying to avoid guilt or sanctimoniousness as we choose between duty and avoidance.

And so my mind wanders as Harry sleeps, blessedly without pain for the moment, moving steadily toward a destination he seems no longer to fear.

He would understand that as we mourn for him, we mourn for ourselves. Of course. We are learning from his dying how to live. We inevitably think of what he did that we can emulate and what we should try to avoid.

And we learn, from his courage and his example, not to fear death. I remember how horrified I was years ago when a mother of a friend of mine, in her late eighties, feeling poorly in the middle of the night, would get up, change into her best nightgown, the one saved for dying, and go back to sleep.

Now I understand. During my last heart attack I had a volcanic desire to live but no fear of dying. It was not at all like my earlier trips to the edge.

Harry continues my education. He did not want trouble while he lived and now he is dying the same way, causing no trouble, trying to smile when he wakes, trying to entertain me.

He needs the comfort of sleep and I leave the room, turning outside his door to see how quickly his eyes close. He wants nothing from us now. Not food, not drink, not, we think, much companionship. He accepts that his road is lonely and he does not even show much impatience at its length.

It is not a happy time, alone in the house with a dying man, but it is not a dreadful time either. I pat the cat who roams the house but will not go to the room where Harry lies; I read, write in my daybook, watch Harry, and take time to celebrate my living.

This house, strange to me, in an unfamiliar city, is filled with silence. No music, no TV, just the quiet in which I can hear his call. But he does not call. I cannot hear his light breathing. Every few minutes I go to the door to see if the covers still rise and fall.

He would understand as I turn from him to watch the tree branch brush the roof of the house next door, as I spend long moments appreciating the dance of shadows from the leaves on the roof, then the patterns of sunlight reflected up on the ceiling of the room where I sit, as I celebrate my remaining life.

Again I stand at the edge of the door watching, waiting, and take instruction from his dying. We should live the hours we have in our own way, appreciating their passing. And we should each die in our own way. I will remember his way, his acceptance, his not giving trouble, his lonely, quiet passing.

This is simple narrative with the facts all true, but it is really not that simple; few things are in writing or in life. The details are selective. A great deal of family history is left out. A great many details about the day, the illness, where it was taking place and why were left out. In fact, I wrote it in part for therapy, and it began as a note to myself several weeks after the experience to help me cut through a jungle of thoughts and emotions, to try to recover for myself what was happening that day. Later I saw that it might speak to others, give comfort or form to their own autobiographies. I did not write the whole truth of that day, although the facts in the piece are accurate; I wrote a limited truth seeking a limited understanding, what Robert Frost called "a momentary stay of confusion."

Yes, I confess it, I wrote, and write, for therapy. Writing autobiography is my way of making meaning of the life I have led and am leading and may lead.

Let's look at another autobiographical poem, one of my favorites, which, I suppose, means that it was one I especially needed to write for no autobiographical reason I can identify. It has not yet been published, although a great many of the best poetry editors in the country have failed in their obligation to Western culture by rejecting it.

BLACK ICE
On the first Saturday of winter, the boy
skated alone on Sailor's Home Pond, circling
from white ice to black, further each time
he rode the thin ice, rising, dipping, bending
the skin of the water until the crack raced
from shore to trick him but he heard, bent
his weight to the turn, made it back in time.

That winter he saw the fish frozen in ice,
its great unblinking eye examining him
each time he circled by. He dreamt that eye
all summer, wondered if Alex had seen
the fish eye before he rode the black ice,

did not hear the crack sneak out from shore,
imagined he learned to skate on water.

At night, after loving you, I fall back
to see that fish eye staring down, watch
Alex in shoe skates and knickers from below
as he skates overhead, circling faster, faster,
scissor legs carrying him from white ice
to black. His skates sing their cutting song,
etching larger, larger circles in my icy sky.

It is true that the boy, myself, skated on thin ice and that he skated at Sailor's Home Pond in Quincy, Massachusetts, although the thin ice may not have been on that pond. He did not, however, see a fish in the ice until he wrote the poem, although he was obsessed with the eyes of the fish, haddock and cod, that followed him when he went to Titus's fish store in Wollaston. Readers believe that Alex is my brother, although I was an only child. There was no Alex; no one I knew had drowned by falling through the ice until I received the poem; I did not, after loving, stare up to see him skating above me until after I wrote the poem. I do now. The poem that was for a few seconds imaginary has become autobiographical by being written.

Ledo Ivo, the Latin American writer, said, "I increasingly feel that my writing creates me. I am the invention of my own words" (Meyer 1989). Don DeLillo explains, "Working at sentences and rhythms is probably the most satisfying thing I do as a writer. I think after a while a writer can begin to know himself through his language. He sees someone or something reflected back at him from these constructions. Over the years it's possible for a writer to shape himself as a human being through the language he uses. I think written language, fiction, goes that deep. He not only sees himself but begins to make himself or remake himself" (LeClair and McCaffery 1988).

We become what we write. That is one of the great magics of writing. I am best known as a nonfiction writer, but I write fiction and poetry to free myself of small truths in the hope of achieving large ones. Here are the first pages from a novel I am writing.

Notebook in his lap, pen uncapped, Ian Fraser sat in the dark green Adirondack chair studying the New Hampshire scene that had so often comforted him as he put in his last years in his Washington office. The green meadow sloping unevenly over granite ledge to the lake and the point of land with its sentinel pine that marked the edge of his possession, and across the lake the hills rising into mountains touched with the reds, oranges, yellows that would flame into autumn this week or next. He was settled in at last and ready to begin the book he had so long delayed, but he could not write until he scanned this quiet scene with his infantryman's eyes for it still was, as were all his land-scapes, a field of fire.

He had to know where to dig in, where the enemy would attack, what was at his back. He supposed it was what had attracted him to this old farmhouse, he could hold this position, he had a good field of fire. First he scanned the lake. Left to right, far edge to near, not one boat or canoe, nothing breaking the surface, no wind trail or wake. Now right to left to see what might be missed. Nothing.

The point of land, his furthest outpost. Scraggly pines, hulking ledge, ideal cover. He studied it close up, knew the pattern of shadows, where the ledge caught the light, where crevice was always dark. This is ridicu-lous, he thought, an old man whose wars are all over, but he could not stop the search for the enemies that had been there at the edge of other fields so long ago, so recent in memory.

The woods left, on the other side from sentinel point. Sweep his eyes at the woods a half a field away, open ground any enemy would have to cross. He made himself still; anyone watching would not know his eyes were on patrol. He could have hidden a platoon in these woods, tree and bush, ledge and rock wall, but there was no shadow that moved, no unexpected sound, no leaves that danced without wind.

And yet, Ian felt a presence as if he, the watcher, were being watched. He scanned the woods on the left again, moving from lake edge up. Nothing.

Now the woods on the right, he had cut back from the house when he bought it, saying he needed sun for vegetables. He needed open field. More hardwoods here, more openness, the road unseen beyond. It was where someone would come in. His flood lights targeted these woods, but it was not night. He examined these familiar woods, suddenly looking high in the old oak where a pileated woodpecker started his machine gun attack. Ian studied squirrel and crow, the pattern of light and dark, followed the trial of the quiet lake breeze that rose through the woods and was gone.

Now the field of fire itself, where a civilian would think no-one could hide. He smiled at the memory of a young paratrooper, himself, home on leave, telling Claire, who would become his first wife, to stand at the top of the field and spot him if she could as he crept up the slope, taking cover where there seemed no cover. She was patient with his soldiering—then. She knew her quarry and did not laugh as this lean young man crawled up the slope moving quickly from ledge to slight hollow to the cover of low bush blueberries that July in 1943.

He never knew if she saw him or not.

Do I have a green lawn that reaches down to a New Hampshire lake? No. Do I still see when I visit a new place, forty-six years after I have been in combat, a good field of fire? Yes. Did I have another wife than Minnie Mae? Yes. Was her name Claire? No. Did I play that silly game in the field when I was home on leave? Yes. Is the setting real? Let Herman Melville answer, "It is not down on any map: true places never are."

What is true, what is documentally autobiographical, in the novel will not be clear to me when I finish the last draft. I confess that at my age I am not sure about the source of most of my autobiography. I have written poems that describe what happened when I left the operating table, looked back and decided to return.

My war stories are constructed of what I experienced, what I heard later, what the history books say, what I needed to believe to survive and recover—two radically different processes.

I dream every night and remember my dreams. Waking is often a release from a greater reality. I read and wear the lives of the characters I inhabit. I do not know where what I know comes from. Was it dreamt, read, overheard, imagined, experienced in life or at the writing desk? I have spun a web more coherent than experience.

But of course I've been talking about fiction, a liar's profession, so let us turn to the realistic world of nonfiction. That novel from which I have quoted is being written, more days than not, by a technique I call layering that I describe in the third edition of *Write to Learn*:

> One technique I've been using, especially in writing the novel, is to layer my writing. Once I did quite a bit of oil painting and my pictures were built up, layer after layer of paint until the scene was revealed to me and a viewer. I've been writing each chapter of the novel the same way, starting each day at the beginning of the chapter, reading and writing until the timer bings and my daily stint is finished. Each day I lay down a new layer of text and when I read it the next day, the new layer reveals more possibility.
>
> There is no one way the chapters develop. Each makes its own demands, struggles towards birth in its own way. Sometimes it starts with a sketch, other times the first writing feels complete [next day's reading usually shows it is not]; sometimes I race ahead through the chapter, other times each paragraph is honed before I go on to the next one. I try to allow the text to tell me what it needs.
>
> I start reading and when I see—or, more likely, hear—something that needs doing, I do it. One day I'll read through all the written text and move it forward from the last day's writing; another time I'll find myself working on dialogue; the next day I may begin to construct a new scene [the basic element of fiction]; one time I'll stumble into a new discovery, later have to set

it up or weave references to it through the text; I may build up background description, develop the conflict, make the reader see a character more clearly; I may present more documentation, evidence, or exposition, or hide it in a character's dialogue or action.

Well, that is academic writing, writing to instruct, textbook writing. It is clearly nonfiction, and to me it is clearly autobiography. And so, I might add, is the research and scholarship that instructs our profession. We make up our own history, our own legends, our own knowledge by writing our autobiography.

This has enormous implications for our students, or should have. In *Notebooks of the Mind*, a seminal book for our discipline, Vera John-Steiner (1985) documents the importance of obsession. "Creativity requires a *continuity of concern*, an intense awareness of one's active inner life combined with sensitivity to the external world." Again and again she documents the importance of allowing and even cultivating the obsessive interest of a student in a limited area of study. I read that as the importance of encouraging and supporting the exploration of the autobiographical themes of individual students—and the importance of allowing ourselves to explore the questions that itch our lives.

I do not think we should move away from personal or reflective narrative in composition courses, but closer to it; I do not think we should limit reflective narrative to a single genre; I do not think we should make sure our students write on many different subjects, but that they write and rewrite in pursuit of those few subjects which obsess them.

But then, of course, I am writing autobiographically, telling other people to do what is important to me.

And so all I can do is just rest my case on my own personal experience. I want to read my most recent poem in which the facts are all true. I had not seen as clearly before I wrote the poem the pattern of those facts, the way I—a generation of children in the United States and Germany and Britain and Japan and China and Spain and France and Italy and Russia and so many other countries—was prepared for war. This piece of writing is factually true but watch out as you hear it. Writing is subversive and something dangerous may happen as you hear my autobiography.

A woman hearing this poem may write, in her mind, a poem of how she was made into a docile helpmate by a society that had its own goals for her. A black listener may write another autobiography as mine is heard but translated by personal history. A person who has been mistreated in childhood, a person who is a Jew, a person whose courage was tested at the urging of jeering peers on a railroad bridge in Missouri, will all hear other poems, write other poems in their mind as they hear mine.

WINTHROP 1936, SEVENTH GRADE
December and we comb our hair wet,
pocket our stocking caps and run,
uniformed in ice helmets,

to read frost etched windows:
castle, moat, battlements, knight,
lady, dragon, feel our sword

plunge in. At recess we fence
with icicles, hide coal in
snow balls, lie freezing

inside snow fort, make ice balls
to arc against the enemy: Hitler.
I lived in a town of Jews,

relatives hidden in silences,
letters returned, doors shut,
curtains drawn. Our soldier

lessons were not in books taught
by old women. In East Boston,
city of Mussolinis, we dance

combat, attack and retreat, sneak,
hide, escape, the companionship
of blood. No school, and side

staggered by icy wind we run
to the sea wall, wait
for the giant seventh wave

to draw back, curl mittens
round iron railing, brace
rubber boots, watch

the entire Atlantic rise
until there is no sky. Keep
mittens tight round iron rail,

prepare for the return of ocean,
that slow, even sucking back,
the next rising wave.

I suspect that when you read my poem, you wrote your own autobiography. That is the terrible, wonderful power of reading: the texts we create in our own minds while we read—or just after we read—become part of the life we believe we lived. Another thesis: all reading is autobiographical.

twenty-three

I Still Wait for the Sheets to Move
(1984)

This is one of Don's best-known essays about his childhood, and reveals much about how he became a writer. He included this essay in early editions of Write to Learn, *showing students how the essay changed from one draft to another.*

I woke in the black New England mornings to a family chore that came before my paper route, and stood in the pale orange of my grandmother's night-light to watch if the sheets rose and fell.

This tall authority of my childhood—a personal acquaintance of God—feared by all the uncles and her daughter, my mother, was now so frail her breathing barely moved the sheets. I tried not to look at the black hole of her mouth—her teeth grinned in a glass on the night table—and studied the top sheet. It did not move. This was the night Grandma died. Just before I decided to wake my parents, the sheet suddenly fluttered and fell.

I first remember Grandma as a great column of skirts and her face looking down, disapproving. Her hair was gathered in a topknot like the crown on Queen Mary, whose picture was in the living room with King George, the Bible, and the gilt-framed steel engravings crated from Scotland and always hung in the front room.

Grandma taught me her own legends. How when she was a schoolgirl in Islay, an island in the Hebrides off Scotland, she had led her friends through the shortcut across the forbidden pasture. I should never disobey as she had disobeyed. Grandma had looked for the bull, but hadn't seen him, and had taken the chance he was not there, as if she had known better than her parents. Then the bull charged.

She shoved her friends behind her, pulled her huge sewing scissors from her schoolbag, and rammed them up the nostrils of the bull.

At the end of the story, she always reminded me to obey my parents, but, of course, I started looking for shortcuts, hoping for bulls.

When I was a child, still living in a single-family house, there was a great porcelain jar in the front hall and, in it, a bouquet of umbrellas and canes. It reminded me of what happened to the robber. It was after Grandmother sailed to America from Scotland for the first time, and when the grandfather I never knew still owned the mill. The payroll was in the safe at the house, and Grandfather was away on business, when Grandma heard someone downstairs.

She found the robber in the kitchen, and he pointed a six-gun at her. She said, "Wait right there." Anyone who knew Grandmother knew he waited. She went to the front hall, selected a heavy cane from the same porcelain jar, returned to the kitchen, broke the robber's wrist with one stroke. Then Grandmother called my Uncle Alec, her oldest son, and told him to fetch the constable.

I never really began to understand why the uncles and my mother were so tied to Grandmother for direction and approval. She certainly gave them direction, but precious little approval. Scots felt duty, obligation, and guilt were better motivators than praise and earthly reward.

While researching this paper I found that Grandma's husband, Morison Smith, whose face looked so sure of itself in the brown photograph on the wall of Grandma's bedroom, had died a failure. Mother and Grandma never let on about that. I was told he had been a mill owner, and he was held up to me as a standard of achievement and proof I belonged in the middle class. But Grandfather, it turns out, lost the mill and lost many other positions. Grandma baked bread to keep the family going. The farm girl from Islay had been a servant girl in London on the command of the absentee landlord, but she escaped that life a decade later by marrying a widower as he left for America to manage a linen mill. Eventually he started his own mill, and she had servants of her own as a mill owner's wife. But he had a "fiddle foot." He was always looking for a better position, a quicker way to become rich. Once he made Grandma cook chocolates on a kitchen stove and he sold them door to door, dreaming he was a Cadbury. Their children saw it was Mother who kept them together as Father failed in America, in England, in Scotland, and then back in America again, where he died, his youngest son still in school.

I despised her pretensions when I was young. We lived in a working-class neighborhood and I could not understand how important it was that we believed we were middle class. She was obsessed with what the neighbors thought. The shades had to be drawn just so, and she changed her clothes every afternoon. We never ate in the kitchen until she was paralyzed and didn't know. Her Sunday dinners were ceremonies, and the family came back for every holiday. She sat at the head of the table.

My mother, my father, my uncle, and I all lived in Grandmother's house, all children always. My mother did not cook, for it was Grandma's kitchen and Grandma's special wood stove; my father, who wore his salesman's smile to work or church, always kept his distance from my grandmother, as if he were still my mother's suitor; my spinster uncle, the accountant, ate his meals quickly, then returned to his account books on the oak desk in the corner of his bedroom; and I took to the streets.

They feared Grandma too much to leave. Our home seemed glued together by fear: fear of God, whose lightning-fast rod was held by Grandma; fear of the neighbors, especially those who were Irish Catholic; fear of Drink, the curse of Scotland; fear of Roosevelt; fear of smoking; fear of sex; fear of failure; fear of having dirty underwear when they take you to the hospital after the accident; fear of being hit by lightning; fear of irregularity and perpetual constipation; fear of food that might poison; fear of the flu that had killed Aunt Helen in 1917; fear of rust that could cause the blood poisoning that left Uncle Alec with a bent finger; fear of the bruise that would become the lump that would become cancer; fear of what you might say and fear of what you might not say; and the greatest fear of all, Grandma.

But she did not entirely terrify me and I don't know why. When I said "darn" she scrubbed out my mouth with laundry soap, and when I tanned in the summer she took the same brown soap and the scrubbing brush she used on the linoleum in the kitchen to scrub the tan away. She believed that "to spare the rod was to harm the child." I was not harmed; her rod was not spared. I was spanked with a shaving strap, with the back of a hairbrush soaked to make it hurt the more, and with my father's hand on my grandmother's command. But I also knew her in a way that her own children did not seem to know her.

When I was young my mother, not allowed to cook or clean in Grandma's house, spent her days with friends, shopping in Boston as if my father owned a mill instead of selling ladies' hosiery. I was alone with Grandma, I sang hymns with her as she did the housework and kept quiet when I heard her talking, casually, with God.

Grandmother was the only one who knew my friends who lived in the walls. She did not talk at them, smiling knowingly and winking over my head; she visited with them. She always remembered the imaginary cake in the invisible pan, and when I painted and repainted the back steps with water, she always knew to step over the wood where the paint had not yet dried. When I tipped over the woven cane living room chairs and covered them with a blanket, she would visit me in the igloo, the cave, the tent. When I lined up the dining room chairs she would sit in the bow and paddle the war canoe, and when I put the fan in front she would fly with me to Paris, as Lindbergh had just done. At the end of the day, when all her chores were done and it was too early to light the lamps and start supper yet too dark to read, she would let me sit with her in the gloaming, sharing her quiet.

Then one Saturday night I rushed up to bed, leaping two steps at a time, and found Grandmother collapsed on the stairs. Her dress moved at last, but she only grunted and could not seem to make sounds with her mouth, now strangely lopsided, and I can still hear myself scream for help.

Late that night, after they had told me time and time again to go to bed and I had paid no attention, long after Dr. Bartlett had gone, we all stood around her bed, where she lay propped halfway up on pillows. I was closest to her on her right side, and when she grew agitated, trying to speak with a terrible animal sound and flailing wildly with her one good arm, I brought her a pad of paper, and I translated the meaning that lay between the scrawled note and the face that was so terribly pulled down on one side. It was I who laughed, and I remember Grandma nodding when I said, "She's telling you when to put the leg of lamb in the oven for Sunday dinner."

Grandma might have suffered a stroke—a shock she would call it—but she would survive, and she would tell us what to do. She lived until she was eighty-nine, another eleven years, and she never got out of bed except when we carried her in a special canvas sling to the couch in the living room for a few awkward holiday dinners that never went right without Grandma in the kitchen.

She grew thin, and her auburn hair that had been gray turned white. Her left arm, which had always been so busy making bread or grape jelly or the thick kidney soup I loved, lay curled and useless outside of the covers, unless we put it in. The skin on that hand grew soft; it was almost transparent, and it had the shiny pale colors I saw on the inside of seashells.

In the early mornings when I went out on my paper route, when I returned for breakfast, when I came home from school, when I came in from playing street hockey, I always checked to see if the sheets still moved. I gave my Victorian grandmother the bedpan when it was needed, I wiped her afterwards, I helped lift her up in the bed, I put salve on her bedsores, and I fed her who had once fed me.

Her physical world shrank to as far as she could reach with her bamboo back-scratcher. She used it to pull up the dark green Black Watch shawl she had brought from Scotland. That back-scratcher is still on my desk. She talked more often with God and lost her sense of time, asking for lunch just after we cleared the luncheon dishes away. But my mother, in her forties and in her fifties, still took daily instruction from Grandma on how to make tea and never felt she did it right.

I went away summers to get tans Grandma could no longer scrub off. At home I had a ceiling of maps—Arabia, Antarctica, Africa, China and Japan—and thought I would leave home. I hung out with the Irish. No one in the family smoked, so I learned to let a cigarette hang from the corner of my mouth, and taught myself to squint my eyes against the smoke. I took that first drink, and then I took more. I ate strange Mediterranean food—spaghetti and ravioli. I ate the pepper and the salads we never served at home, and went off to college to play football and to think I had left Grandma and my family forever.

The last time I saw Grandmother I was a paratrooper going overseas to fight Hitler. I stood by my grandmother's bed and she smiled her crooked smile and held my hand with her good right hand, terribly weak now. She knew I was going off to war, but as we talked I realized I was not this Donald going off to World War II or Donald, her son, who was in the Navy in the First World War, or Donald her father, or Donald her brother, but Donald her great-uncle who had sat around the fire when she was a girl in the 1860s, and shown off the bent leg that had taken a ball at Waterloo. And with that bringing together that the elderly can do, spanning centuries in a second, I became the lad going off to fight Napoleon.

Grandma died in a letter I received when I was hiding from shellfire in the rubble of a German city, but I knew by then I would never really leave home, that I would never live without the sense of death nearby. Now I have, like Grandma, buried my father, my mother, and a daughter. I live to more of her standards than I like to admit, and when I wake early or come home late it is first with a sense of dread. I stand in the shadows of the upstairs hall, watching the ones I love, to see if the sheets will move.

If you want to take a year off to write a book, you have to **take** that year, or the year will take you by the hair and pull you toward the grave...you can take your choice. You can keep a tidy house, and when St. Peter asks you what you did with your life, you can say, I kept a tidy house, I made my own cheese balls.
                                          — *Annie Dillard*

The art of the novel is getting the whole thing written.
                                          — *Leonard Gardner*

I believe that the so-called "writing block" is a product of some kind of disproportion between your standards and your performance... one should lower his standards until there is no felt threshold to go over in writing. It's **easy** to write. You just shouldn't have standards that inhibit you from writing... I can imagine a person beginning to feel he's not able to write up to that standard he imagines the world has set for him. But to me that's surrealistic. The only standard I can rationally have is the standard I'm meeting right now...You should be more willing to forgive yourself. It doesn't make any difference if you are good or bad today. The **assessment** of the product is something that happens **after** you've done it. — *William Stafford*

Living's hard. It's writing that's easy. — *E. Annie Proulx*

twenty-four

The Importance of Making Snow
(1985)

Don wrote this piece during a graduate seminar in 1985 that focused on creativity and the writing process. "The Importance of Making Snow" was one of Don's weekly responses, quick pieces that the seminar participants wrote and read to each other.

I write because I can not not write. Yet I have responsibilities, obligations, duties, demands, appointments that require attention and I do not write; I suffer a lack of faith, of quiet, of listening time, of confidence in what I may say and do not write; I think intellectually or aesthetically about what I might write, debating what I may say and how I may say it—shopping this genre, that voice, this structure, that point of view,—and do not write; I tell myself that I have no need to be compulsive, that I should let the field lay fallow for a season and do not write. Then my muse, who was a Greek dish with come-on eyes when I was young, a gal who wore a filmy robe and had cute little fluttery wings, has grown as thick in the waist as I have, wears a moustache, an off-the-rack denim gown, and her wings droop beyond her buttocks. No come-on looks anymore, she tells me to write with a cramping kick in the bowels, often delivered while I sleep.

As if I needed her to tell me to write. What does she think I've been telling myself? I know I have lost the gift of concentration and the ability to select the significant from the trivial; all tasks become equally important and equally impossible. I am harried, pressured, irritable and despairing. Strangers look at my face and ask me if I am alright. I start to tell them just how bad I am and they move away. Friends and family edge away from me. I want more love and understanding and compassion than a battalion of concubines and a regiment of Freuds could deliver. I pass through self pity and achieve despair.

And then, since it is all hopeless—the letters will never be answered, the manuscripts never read, the classes and the meetings and the talks never properly prepared, the obligatory books and articles never read—I tell myself I might as well write. Sometimes it takes a paragraph, but most times it is a sentence or two, perhaps only a line, and I am within the act of writing once more.

I feel again what I seek most in writing, the quiet that is at the center of the writing act. It is a strange kind of quiet for although I sometimes stare trancelike watching bark grow on the tall pine outside my writing room window, more often my quiet is entirely internal. The radio blares music in my office or the world careens by me while I sit in car or on rock wall or at restaurant table, my fingers attack the word processor keyboard or my pen scuttles across the page, but I am lost to all worlds outside of the writing. Everything I am is concentrated on the task of listening to the words that will land on the page and line themselves up in interesting order.

There is always magic in this for me, and wonder because I do not know what I am going to say until it is said. The writer within is always a stranger, with a grin, a top hat and long, quick fingers which produce what was not there the moment before. I shall never know this magic man well, although he has been within me for sixty years. He entices me with his capacity to surprise.

We've been a pretty good team, all told, the surpriser and the surprised. We are children of the Great Depression and we appreciate the very fact of work. And it has been good work, jobs that are a challenge but not impossible. Better than that it has been serious work for the most part, the kind of work that contributes to society in its own way. We escaped the Evangelical Church to become evangelicals of a different order, preaching through editorials and textbooks. Still that aging magician, fingers gnarled and slower now, moustache white, joints creaking, sneaks out of the house late at night, when he didn't think I am watching, and dances naked in imaginary moonlight, trying steps he never could perform.

He's been a good companion and I will not laugh. I realize that the morning after he has tried to do what can not be done, he shows no sense of failure. He appears elated, serene, and smiles as if he had just said something clever to himself. In fact, he seems most depressed when he performs, with flawless craft, what we both knew could be done. The audience cheers, he bows and waves, but spends the days afterwards kicking at pigeons, grunting, groaning, and talking about applying to the Magicians' Home in Farmington.

When he mopes about, he doesn't get much sympathy from those who can't get an invitation to perform at the Dover KofC Spring Stag Festival. He feels guilty grousing because he is doing O.K. He has not one top hat but seven, plenty of rabbits, a roomful of gaily colored ribbons.

Of course he takes pride in his craft but he has learned to do his best tricks blindfolded or backwards or with unexpected props. One night I saw him borrow Tom Romano's beret and pull out a thick crust pizza with everything out of it. The magician tries to find content in the small pleasures of his art, the triangular folding of the silk squares, the setting of the wire release, the warm-up ruffles of the cards but all he feels is guilty discontent.

He even has security, a trick few magicians can ever pull off. He has tenure and plenty of interesting apprentices at Magician U. His students play at Las Vegas, appear on the Johnny Carson Show, one even made Casper Weinberger laugh at a White House gala. He enjoys seeing students come in wondering if they could ever be magicians. He smiles and invites them to teach him their tricks and, with the master watching, their fingers know tricks the students' didn't know they knew. It's good work and the old man knows it, but still he wants to watch his own fingers do things he doesn't know they can do.

That old fellow has lost failure. Even if the doves do not flutter and fly out of the hat, he knows how to make the mistake appear it was a calculated part of the act. He fills empty spots with patter and deflects the heckler with a glib retort. He's a pro. He shows up on time, is willing to follow dog acts, can play straight man to the comic starting out. He'll be booked for next season and yet. . . .

He wants me to assign him bigger challenges. Just when he should be reaping, he wants to sow. He is filled with dreams of what can't be done and are of no use if they can. He didn't start out to be a magician after all. He planned to be a realtor before he found someone else used the name. As a boy, he wanted to make fantasy as real as it was to him. He was sad when others read the books he had read and did not have the characters walk off the pages into their lives.

He knew, if he worked hard, he could make fantasy real. A snap of the fingers and the coffin opens and the husband, laughing, runs to his wife. The soldiers' bullets become ice cream cones that arc right into the hands of the enemy. The deer sneak up on the hunters and tickle them until they drop their guns. Eat too much and you become thin. Sing and the notes are there. Flap your ears and fly. Dance and the orchestra in the privet hedge begins to play.

O.K., Magician. You've earned your keep. Now it's time to play. And don't forget to work on Jane Hansen's private snow storm, six feet square, so she can ski to work in July. Tom wants one, too? Make her snow storm six by twelve but he has to stay in second place. What if the old magician fails? He smiles knowing it is better to create snow that will not fall, than never to have created snow at all.

nulla dies sine linea
Never a day without a line

– Horace 65-8 B.C.

Afterword

In the spring of 1997, the National Council of Teachers of English, meeting in Charlotte, North Carolina, paid tribute to Don Murray and his work.

I was honored to speak about Don, my longtime mentor and friend. I was part of Don's journalism family, comprising hundreds of reporters and editors, students and professionals alike, who learned from Don how to better write and, perhaps more importantly, how to coach others to do the same. I'm fairly certain I was the only newspaper reporter in the standing-room-only crowd.

From the podium, I gazed out at the crowd of English professors, composition teachers, and other academicians there to talk about Don's enduring contributions to their fields of study.

Seeing you all, I told the group, is "like finding that all these years your father has had another family besides yours."

The relationship between journalists and professors is usually a frosty one; each side remains convinced the other is irrelevant to their work. Don Murray crossed the divide. Tall and brawny, the onetime football player, World War II paratrooper, and military policeman, newspaper reporter, Pulitzer Prize winner for editorial writing, English and journalism professor, consulting and writing coach, Don was a giant with one foot planted in the newsroom, and the other firmly set in the schools.

In *The Essential Don Murray*, two of Don's colleagues at the University of New Hampshire, Thomas Newkirk and Lisa Miller, link Don's outsized presence in two fields that fueled his passion for making meaning with words.

They were able to do so because of yet another gift from Don: the donation of his collected papers to The Poynter Institute, the school for journalists in St. Petersburg, Florida. Like UNH, Poynter is one of the many institutions where Don preached his gospel of the writing process: writing may be magical but it's not magic. It's a process, a rational series of decisions and steps that every writer makes and takes, no matter what the length, the deadline, even the genre, from dissertation to feature story, from screenplay to police brief.

I first heard Don express this philosophy in 1981, as a reporter for *The Providence Journal*, when Don was hired to be the paper's writing coach. Until then, my process resembled more of a feverish, anxiety-ridden race from assignment to deadline.

Until then, I had grown up believing just the opposite, the myth that enshrouds the process; writing had everything to do with magic; to be a great writer you had to be a magician, a God, or at least a genius—preferably one who received regular visits from a Muse.

From that moment, Don's process approach transformed the way I thought and wrote; it represents the single most important element of my education as a writer and subsequently as a teacher, an influence so powerful it transformed me into a disciple dedicated to spreading his word as often and far as possible.

Soon after that first workshop, I wrote a fan letter to Don, who invited my wife Kathy and me to spend Easter weekend at his house in Durham with him and Minnie Mae.

We soon learned that Minnie Mae was not just his wife during a marriage that lasted more than five decades but his partner; she was the one who typed Don's early articles. Don never tired of telling how Minnie Mae helped launch his freelance career, by fishing out a manuscript Don had dumped in the trash and submitting it to a magazine. The magazine published the story.

That Easter Sunday nearly three decades ago, I woke up early to find Don sitting in his Morris chair on the Murrays' screened-in porch, sipping from a mug of his favorite China Black tea. He had already written a poem about an incident in World War II; exhausted and hungry, he sat down on a log to eat his K-rations, only to discover the "seat" was the corpse of a chaplain.

The poem is one of hundreds of items in the Murray collection, filling more than 100 archival boxes held in Poynter's Eugene Patterson Library, where they have found shelter under the guidance of library director David Shedden and curator Jean Wood, who oversees Don's papers with dedication, skill, and grace.

I had already seen many of its contents before they became part of the collection; Don gave me the honor of being an early reader (Minnie Mae, of course, had pride of place) of much of the collection's contents: handouts, timelines, daybook entries, biographical timelines, word counts, a slew of laminated cards bearing testimony from other writers, drafts and published versions of speeches, articles, newspaper columns and books, chapter by chapter, and finally the books themselves. Don also shared interviews and stories with other writers who fueled our work. Others in his extended family were other recipients.

What began that Easter as a classic mentor-protégé relationship grew, to my great fortune, into an enduring friendship between two writers passionate about how good writing was made.

We corresponded by mail, then email and phone calls, often calling each other several times a day. Less frequent but no less cherished are the times we spent together. We exchanged drafts, revised, resent. We shared our personal and literary ups and downs, many times sending a manuscript topped with a bulleted list of questions: "Should I give up writing? Is this crap?" When I begin teaching at Poynter, Don was guide, sometimes daily.

I can't imagine a more fruitful relationship, one that lasted until Don's death, at age 82, on December 30, 2006. As with the makers of this book and its audience, Don is a presence we mourn every day. *The Essential Don Murray* provides solace by capturing on the page how he inspired, influenced, and loved us.

As a writing teacher or teaching writer (we debated the correct description of our role) I learned from a master, through the contents of this book and, to my immense luck, from the man himself—about professionalism, generosity, the joy of reading, and learning by teaching others.

I don't want to give the impression that I was the only protégé/friend in his life; I was one of many, in Durham and elsewhere. His wife Minnie Mae and daughters, Anne and Hannah, their families, and his grandchildren blessed his days. He had his early morning crowd at The Bagelry, enthusiastic readers of his deeply personal *Boston Globe* column, which explored aging through the prism of his personal life, and many friends and colleagues.

His UNH journalism students returned to him time and again for career advice and shared their books and other achievements. The same went for Don's other family, the writing teachers who filled that conference room in North Carolina twelve years ago. If someone wrote to him about writing, Don typically showered all comers with his articles and books. I can't remember him turning down an invitation to speak, or be interviewed.

Don's death left a hole in many hearts. The samples of his prodigious output on display in this collection provide testimony to the power of the writing process and his commitment to never let a day go by without a line written. Don bequeathed a legacy of creativity, professionalism, and humility toward his craft that brings both of his professional families together. In this case, *The Essential Don Murray* is magical and magic.

Chip Scanlan
Senior Faculty—Writing
The Poynter Institute

Origins

"Teach Writing as Process Not Product" was first published in *The Leaflet*, Fall 1972, pp. 11–14 (New England Association of Teachers of English).

"Writing as Process: How Writing Finds Its Own Meaning" was first published in 1980 in *Eight Approaches to Teaching Composition*, edited by Timothy R. Donovan and Ben W. McClelland (National Council of Teachers of English).

"Write Before Writing" was first published in *College Composition and Communication* in December 1978.

Various pages from some of Don Murray's many daybooks

"Listening to Writing" was originally published in *Composition and Teaching* in December 1980.

"Voice of the Text" was a handout in an advanced nonfiction course Don taught.

"Getting Under the Lightning" was first published in 1985 in *Writers on Writing*, edited by Tom Waldrep (Random House).

"Teaching the Other Self: The Writers' First Reader" was first published in *College Composition and Communication* in May 1982.

"Like Orwell, Essaying One's Best" was an Over 60 column that appeared January 17, 1995, in the *Boston Globe*.

"Writing Badly to Write Well: Searching for the Instructive Line" originally appeared in 1984 in *Sentence Combining: A Rhetorical Perspective*, edited by Donald A. Daiker, Andrew Kerek, and Max Morenberg (Southern Illinois University Press).

"A Writer's Canon Revised" was an undated handout.

The "Notes for Discussion" handout was prepared for Paul Matsuda's Creative Nonfiction Class at UNH, April 17, 2002.

"Internal Revision: A Process Discovery" appeared in 1978 in *Research on Composing—Points of Departure*, edited by Charles R. Cooper and Lee Odell (National Council of Teachers of English).

"Don—Still the Copy Editor" shows the first page of *One Writer's Notes*, which was used as a course handout.

"The Listening Eye: Reflections on the Writing Conference" was first published in the Spring 1979 issue of *College English* (vol. 41, pp. 232–237).

"Don Drawing Don" appeared on the first page of a handout of his article "The Teaching Craft: Telling, Listening, Revealing," published in *English Education* (vol. 14, issue 1) in February 1982. The article was adapted from a speech Don gave November 21, 1981, at the NCTE convention in Boston.

"One Writer's Secrets" appeared in the May 1986 edition of *College Composition and Communication* (vol. 37, no. 2, pp. 146–153).

"Where Was I Headed When I Left?" was one of Don's contributions to a graduate course he taught on writing methods.

"A Writer's Geography—One Writer at Work," was a handout for a course Don taught at the University of Colorado, dated September 19, 1991. This was adapted from a speech he had given.

"Notes on Narrative Time" was a handout for the January 29, 2002, UNH Freshman English staff meeting.

"Two Poems": "Minnie Mae Cooks a Poem" was published in 1995 in *All That Matters* by Linda Rief (Heinemann); "Back Row, Sixth Grade" was published in 1990 in *The Writing Teacher as Researcher: Essays in the Theory and Practice of Class-Based Research*, edited by Donald Daiker and Max Morenberg (Boynton/Cook).

"All Writing Is Autobiography" appeared in the February 1991 issue of *College Composition and Communication* (vol. 42, no. 1).

"I Still Wait for the Sheets to Move" was published in early editions of *Write to Learn*.

"The Importance of Making Snow" was one of Don's contributions to a graduate course he taught on writing methods.

Works Cited

Chomsky, Carol. 1971. "Write First, Read Later." *Childhood Education* 47 (6): 296–99.

Emig, Janet. 1971. *The Composing Processes of Twelfth Graders.* Urbana, IL: National Council of Teachers of English.

———. 1975. "The Biology of Writing: Another View of the Process." In *The Writing Processes of Students*, eds. W. T. Petty and P. J. Finn. Buffalo: State University of New York, Department of Elementary and Remedial Education.

Getzels, Jacob W., and Mihaly Csikszentmihalyi. 1976. *The Creative Vision: A Longitudinal Study of Problem-Finding in Art.* New York: John Wiley & Sons.

Graves, Donald. 1975. "An Examination of the Writing Processes of Seven Year Old Children." *Research in the Teaching of English* 9: 227–41.

———. 1978. *Balance the Basics: Let Them Write.* New York: Ford Foundation.

John-Steiner, Vera. 1985. *Notebooks of the Mind.* Albuquerque: University of New Mexico Press.

LeClair, Tom, and Larry McCaffery, eds. 1988. *Anything Can Happen.* Champaign: University of Illinois Press.

Lenz, Siegfried. [1968] 1971. *The German Lesson.* New York: Hill and Wang.

McCrimmon, James. 1950. *Writing with a Purpose.* Boston: Houghton Mifflin.

Meyer, Doris, ed. 1989. *Lives on the Line*. Berkeley: University of California Press.

Murray, Donald M. 1984. *Write to Learn*. New York: Holt, Rinehart & Winston.

———. 1985. *A Writer Teaches Writing: A Complete Revision*. Boston: Houghton Mifflin.

———. 1987. *Write to Learn*. 2d ed. New York: Holt McDougal.

———. 1995. *Write to Learn*. 3d ed. Clifton Park, NY: Delmar.

———. 2003. *The Lively Shadow: Living with the Death of a Child*. New York: Ballantine.

Orwell, Sonia, and Ian Angus, eds. 1968. *Collected Essays, Journalism and Letters of George Orwell*. New York: Harcourt, Brace & World.

Perl, Sondra. 1979. "Unskilled Writers as Composers." *New York University Education Quarterly* 10 (3/Spring): 18–22.

Plimpton, George. 1974. "Interview with Joseph Heller." *The Paris Review* (Winter): 126–47.

Stafford, William. 1978. *Writing the Australian Crawl*. Ann Arbor: University of Michigan Press.